CW01660639

WHISTLEDON

Bryn Berry

Copyright © Bryn Berry 2025 All rights reserved.

This is a work of fiction. Names, characters, businesses, places, events, locales, and incidents are either the products of the author's imagination or used in a fictitious manner. Any resemblance to actual persons, living or dead, or actual events is purely coincidental.

ISBN 978-1-0682432-0-2

Dardy Publishing

2025

For Elsie and Wilfred

"No man ever steps in the same river twice, for it is not the same river and he is not the same man."

(Heraclitus of Ephesus c. 540 – c.480 BCE)

"I will greet this day with love in my heart. And how will I do this? Henceforth will I look on all things with love. And I will be born again. I will love the sun for it warms my bones; yet I will love the rain, for it cleanses the spirit. I will love the light for it shows me the way; yet I will love the darkness, for it shows me the stars. I will welcome happiness, for it enlarges my heart; yet I will endure sadness, for it opens my soul. I will acknowledge rewards for they are my due; yet I will welcome obstacles, for they are my challenge."

(Og Mandino. (1923)

Acknowledgements

Many thanks to editors Jessica Webster and Heather Evans for their thorough reading.

Bryn is very grateful for the support of family members, who have lived in the world of Whistledon for the past few years. (Sometimes querying Bryn's sanity.)

Characters

Sir Charles Fairweather, Baronet
Lady Elspeth Fairweather, his wife
Katrina, their daughter
Angus. their son,
Gertrude Robinson, housekeeper
Clive Robinson chauffeur/handyman
Bill Bates, gardener
Toby, Angus' ex RAF friend
Rodney, groom
Robbie Farquhar, Elspeth's brother
Fiona Farquhar, Robbie's wife
Bishop Dominic Gregory, Angus' godfather
Reverend Simon Shorthouse, rector
Claire Shorthouse, his wife
Dinah, their daughter
Canon Huw Lloyd
Kris Lewis, curate

Prologue

The Reverend Simon Shorthouse watches the men heave the grand piano, shrouded in blankets, into the van, for the short journey back to the Hall. Satisfied with the instrument's safety, he returns to the church as the first clear notes of Purcell's Trumpet Tune swell out.

He sinks into the nearest pew and closes his eyes, allowing the music to envelop him for a few minutes.

Standing, he makes his way to the organ where the young man's hands are excitedly pushing and pulling the stops, his feet moving rapidly over the wooden pedals.

Simon isn't surprised that the organ refurbishment has been expedited in time for the funeral. Bishop Gregory was at Harrow School with Charles, quid pro quo. The Fairweathers have always been generous in support of the church. Simon doubts that he can expect similar backing from Angus. He hopes Lady F will prompt her son. There's nothing like the sound of reverberating organ pipes to stir the congregation into song and cover up their musical imperfections; at least they have a go, join in. Is he serving them well enough? Difficult when his hands are tied by outdated practices. Attendance numbers are falling, but they are falling everywhere.

The villagers are in shock; he wants to bring comfort and hope. Calming, uplifting music will help. The last notes fade away; the organist looks up.

'Morning. Simon. So much better, so much better.'

Simon smiles, the church seems brighter.

1

Whistledon on Wye

September 1970

The hearse draws up by the lychgate. Elspeth Fairweather, elegant in a black silk dress, eases herself out of the following Bentley, stands erect, head held high. Dark-suited estate workers shoulder the flower-bedecked coffin. The slow procession begins. Angus, lightly holding his mother's arm, guides her to the church porch. The waiting rector turns, leading the way. The voices of the church choir soar. "Praise my soul the king of heaven".

Elspeth, face impassive, allows her eyes to flick from side to side, looking, not making contact. She repeats the mantra "Everything is as it should be" until she shivers at the sight of a slim figure, a head of dark hair silvering at the temples, seated at the end of a pew. She shifts her gaze to the bronze chrysanthemums on Charles' coffin. Thank goodness Dominic is here. He will help to ensure the service has the right tone.

At the front of the crowded church, her heart is beating wildly, the pew unforgiving under her sitting bones, Katrina's thigh fleshy against hers. She feels alone, missing Charles by her side. Clutching the Order of Service with his photograph to her heart brings comfort, until the vision of his bleeding body strikes her memory. She stiffens, returns to the mantra, fighting off thoughts of Istanbul.

Dominic is praising Charles, praising her too, saying how they had been a wonderful couple, helping each other over the years. She flinches, she could have been better, but so could Charles. Anger sweeps through her body, Charles should not have been meeting that woman, he should be here now, running the estate. She fumbles in her black patent bag, pulls out a handkerchief, wipes away the tears running down her cheeks. Dominic, holding his bishop's crosier, steps down from the lectern, shoulders bowed, walks across to his seat. Angus is striding across to the podium, his notes in hand. She hears him speaking of his father - a numbness descends. It's all a bad dream. She catches a glance from Dominic to the rector; he stands, makes his way to the pulpit. She wonders if the rector is comfortable dealing with the upper classes, including members of the Diplomatic Service. He should have seated all of them in the permanent pews, instead of those folding canvas chairs. She ought to have taken charge herself. She hopes he will keep it short, won't mention his left-wing leanings. The owners of the expensive vehicles in the church car park won't want to hear his pacifist thoughts. He is gripping the sides of the lectern, turning his head looking at them shuffling on the temporary chairs.

‘Dear Lord, I ask you to comfort Elspeth, Angus, Katrina, their family and friends in this time of grief. Sudden, violent death happens every day in many areas. Each death shakes the connected families, friends and colleagues. Today, we remember Charles as he lived with us. We thank You for his contribution to the diplomatic world, and to village life, here, in Whistledon-on-Wye. We mourn his passing, grieve his loss, but know that his spirit lives on.’ He nods to the choirmaster.

A single tenor voice rings out as the procession to the churchyard begins. Elspeth, following, shudders at the sight of the deep, gaping hole, deep enough for another. Listening as the rector intones the burial words, she watches the coffin being lowered. She is aware of Angus bending, picking up a handful of earth, dropping it on top of the coffin. Her eyes fill with tears. The finality of the moment overcomes her. A gentle touch on her shoulder. Katrina is by her side. ‘I think we need to lead the way to the church hall.’

Elspeth gives her daughter a grateful smile.

‘That seemed to go as well as could be expected.’ Angus is standing beside them, sounding at ease and confident.

The caterers have decorated the tables with small posies of flowers. The smell of ham and egg sandwiches pervades the air. The clatter of plates and the hissing steam from the tea urn are intrusive after the peace and serenity of the church.

A small queue forms to offer condolences. She wants to take the whisky flask out of her handbag, but the pressure is relentless.

The villagers have turned out in force; Charles was popular. The handshake is firm; an elderly man looks at her gravely, eyes concerned. His legs are extremely long in their well-tailored black trousers. She wonders if he has a wife and what she is like. She gives him a carefully controlled smile: not too much, not too little. Charles will be sleeping more easily knowing justice has been done. She turns to the next in line; he is much younger with a chubby face, full of himself, still learning his trade. The Diplomatic Service attracts some odd people; she will be glad when they have all taken themselves off. It is a pity that Katrina is readying herself to go, needing to get back to the children.

Elspeth looks at Dominic slumped in the armchair; there is a gentle snoring sound, his head has dropped, his eyes are closed. She sighs; it's been a long day. The poor fellow is exhausted: he's lost his oldest friend and has had to bury him. She looks at him fondly, the bald patch on the top of his head, the peaceful expression on his face. Since first meeting Charles, he has always been there; they've had some good times together. She blinks the tears away.

Angus has disappeared to the stables; everyone else has gone. It is too quiet. She opens the front door, stands, watches a cloud of starlings going home to roost; her eyes follow them until they disappear. Stepping out towards the walled garden, her thoughts return to the men from the Foreign Office and how crass they were today, talking of plots and terrorism. Why couldn't they have kept their thoughts to themselves? This should have been Charles' day, the focus on him.

The evening is cool; she pulls her cardigan closely around her, watches the orange-tinged sky darkening. She used to stand beside Charles, sharing the magnificence of glorious sunsets. Her heart is heavy. She remembers the text used by the rector: "Let not your heart be troubled." Easier said than done. Then, "In my Father's house there are many mansions." She hopes Charles is happy, wherever he is. Does she believe in an afterlife? Perhaps rebirth: she can't think that Charles isn't somewhere. She gives her head a little shake; better move on.

Entering the walled garden, she sighs. There is a gnawing ache in her body, she needs to find peace. Can she find it in the beauty around her? The apples ripening against the walls, the bricks glowing in the setting sun. She crosses to the chrysanthemums, cradles the curled bronze petals. One breaks off, drops into her hand. She lets it fall to the ground.

Staring at it, a prickly sensation begins at her toes, creeps up her legs to her buttocks and spine. Sudden anxiety surfaces; she stamps her feet to rid herself of the disquiet. Is she being watched? Is someone following her? Glancing behind, she thinks she can see a pale shadowy figure staring at her. She watches, transfixed; it turns and walks away, disappearing through the gathering dusk. She is panting, can't move. Was it him? Her blood chills, she has brought this on herself. She is being punished. No! It is a trick of her imagination; she is overwrought. She needs to get back to Dominic. She sets off, hears her footsteps ringing out, no other sound. The birds have reached their roosts; she can make out a pale quarter-moon. A single owl hoots in the distance. She walks steadily, deliberately, towards the front door.

Dominic, still in the chair, opens his eyes as she comes in, blinks, then looks at her, encouragingly. She can't tell anyone; they will think she's going mad. Or is she? Does she believe in ghosts? She doesn't know. She moves towards the row of decanters on the cabinet, selects a whisky.

Dominic stands, 'Let me pour. We can both do with a pick-me-up.'

His hand on her shoulder is reassuring. She gives it a responsive squeeze. 'I think I will take mine to my room.'

Elspeth awakes with an uneasy feeling in her belly, she lies eyes closed, breathing into the sensation, remembers the figure turning towards her. Was it really a ghost? Do they exist? Should she tell Dominic? Does Dominic know about apparitions?

Getting dressed, she loses her balance, sits on the edge of the bed to fasten her blouse. She must pull herself together. Dare she tell him?

He's already at breakfast; looking up from the toast he's buttering, a broad welcoming smile changes to a frown. 'Good morning, Elspeth. Did you manage to sleep?'

'A little.' She takes a deep breath; how much should she tell him? 'Do you believe in ghosts?'

He sits back, eyebrows raised. 'Well, yes, I do. Why do you ask?'

Gertrude, bustling in with fresh tea, stops in her tracks. She puts the tray on the table and hurries out.

'I think I saw one last night.'

Dominic's eyes narrow. 'Have there been sightings before?'

'I don't know. Charles always played down stories about the supernatural.'

'His work gave him enough to think about. If he had seen an apparition himself, he might have taken more interest.'

Dominic pushes his chair back, stands, walks to her side. His hand is comforting as he helps her into her chair. She sits with her elbows on the table, forehead resting on clenched fists. His voice is soft, his tone measured. 'Can you tell me what you saw?'

She looks up at him; his face is calm. He is waiting for her to say something. What can she tell him?

'It looked like a man. He wasn't very clear. He seemed to dissolve into the wall.'

'Did you recognise him? Are you able to tell me who it was?'

'I'm not sure. It wasn't Charles.'

'It is nothing to worry about, simply that the poor soul needs to transition. I'm sure the Church can help.

2

The floor is cold. Simon quickly pushes his feet into his slippers. Claire is lying looking at him out of half-closed eyes.

'Got to crack today's sermon.' He pulls on his dressing gown and pads across to the window. Opening the curtains, he frowns at the water pooling on the path, the roses sagging limply. 'That's a pity. It's raining.'

'It might not keep them away. A lot of them have said how shaken they feel.'

'Yes,' He turns to look at her, 'yet others don't seem to give a toss.'

She sits up. 'It's unlikely those people would ever come to a Sunday Service.'

'You're right. What troubles me the most is the hatred I've heard from people who regularly attend. I'm obviously not getting my message across.'

'You'd better get to it then.' Laughing, she slides back under the covers.

He grins, ignoring the temptation to get back into bed.

As Simon enters the kitchen, the dogs stretch and drop from their sofa; he opens the back door, nudges them out. They soon return, shaking the rain from their coats before snuggling down again. He heads for his study, wanting to get his thoughts on paper whilst they are fresh, and the world is quiet.

He'll make the point that violence is not what God wants, from anybody, however justified they may feel it is. Compassion is the key. Shall he mention the Crusades? He holds his breath. Something's wrong with not permitting any violence. He was glad he hadn't killed anyone in the war. Other people had done that for him. He's free, lucky. He has no way of knowing what part diplomacy played in his freedom. Why did someone shoot Charles? As much as he dislikes the heritage of the Fairweather family, the present ones are not responsible for the crimes committed in the past and, like all humans, feel pain of loss.

As he finalises the sermon, the smell of bacon frying prompts him to hurry upstairs to shower.

'I bet he was up to something,' Claire puts the breakfast in front of him.

'Who? Charles?'

She nods. 'Everybody knows the upper class like to feather their own nests. You've only got to visit a stately home to see the ornaments and sculptures they've brought back.'

Raising his eyebrows, he looks at her sternly. 'The poor chap might just have been doing his job. Diplomacy can't be easy when there's so much unrest.'

She slices her black pudding, spears it and dips it into her mustard.

It isn't a bad turnout, considering the weather. Climbing the steps to the pulpit, Simon is aware of whispering. He half expected it. He clears his throat and projects his voice,

'Thou shalt not kill. The sixth commandment is at the foundation of our religion, and most other religions too.' His gaze encompasses the whole congregation. 'Jesus said "turn the other cheek." He also said that God forgives sinners. This morning, we pray for all the victims, and the perpetrators of violence.' His eye catches Lady Fairweather's. She is looking at him intently. 'Bitterness eats away at the bitter; they need to forgive. We ask for forgiveness, and we forgive.'

In the porch, Elspeth, taking the outstretched hand of the rector, avoids meeting his eyes. She smiles and, holding herself tall, turns to walk quickly out of the church grounds.

"Thou shalt not kill." It's all very well for him to lecture but sometimes you must be practical, pragmatic. That's why moleskins are hanging on the fence and crows dangling by their feet, proudly displayed by the farmers protecting the crops. Does

Claire swat flies when they come around the food? Do they have one of those unpleasant sticky papers hanging in the kitchen? Repentance and forgiveness aren't always appropriate. The memory of the figure in the walled garden crosses her mind; she pushes the thought away. She needs to find something to do; there is too much time to think.

Perhaps she'll accept Robbie's invitation to Scotland, back to people who know that shooting is part of life. If it hadn't been for a shooting party, she might never have met Charles.

Simon throws off his cassock. He wishes it was just as simple to remove the uneasy feeling that has been sitting in his gut since Lady F fixed her gaze on him. Afterwards, she'd shaken his hand and thanked him, but she would as a matter of courtesy. He's a fool; it was clumsy to directly raise the topic of killing so soon after Charles' death, especially when she was amongst the congregation. 'God, please guide me to be more sensitive to other people's needs.'

3

Whistledon on Wye

1951

Angus flicks his blond hair out of his eyes. Books, books and more books, all neatly stacked on the shelves which are on every wall. He sighs long and deeply.

"You must read widely," they keep saying. Grandfather, a book open on his knee, is fast asleep, the brandy bottle close at hand. Angus tiptoes out of the room; he'll saddle Annabel for a ride across the fields to the river.

The sun is blazing down from a blue sky; vapour trails make criss-cross patterns amongst the scudding white clouds. He is happy to allow the horse to set the pace. Soon she is standing in the shallow water at the river's edge. Looking back up the hill, Angus can see the stone-built Hall, the stables at the side and trees rising behind it. He doubts the man responsible for its construction, his ancestor Captain Morgan Fairweather, was told to read widely; he'd done well by importing rum from the West Indies. Angus gives

Annabel a pat, then urges her on for a gallop along the riverbank to the village.

Reaching the church and its rectory, he slows, carefully avoiding the roots of the old yew trees. The graveyard is in shadow, casting a chill in the air as they skirt around it. Annabel's ears prick up. Angus shivers. Turning, he retraces the path; it is time for tea with Grandpa.

Buenos Aries

Elspeth kicks off her high heeled shoes and plants her bare feet firmly on the cool tiles. It has been a hot summer and, although the weather is cooling down, it is humid and sticky. She is glad to be able to relax for a while with nobody judging her. There, on the side table, is a rare sight, a letter from Angus. She picks it up eagerly.

Upper Whistledon Hall

Dear Ma and Pa,

I hope that you both had a good Easter in Buenos Aires. It's been great here. We went to the races at Chepstow on Wednesday. I've done a lot of riding. Grandpa is glad to have help with the horses. I'll be back at school next week. I'm thinking of joining the ATC. I've decided I want to be a pilot.

Love,

Angus

How will Charles react to the news? He expects Angus to follow in the family footsteps and find a career in the Diplomatic Service. She has never been sure of that. Angus has always been able to surprise people with things that he does and says. However, this is a bolt out of the blue. If he had said that he wanted to become a farmer and take over some of the family land or go overseas to get experience of different ways of farming, she would not have been surprised. This idea of his becoming a pilot is a shock.

She finds Charles in his study.

'Oh, my goodness! Listen to this. In fact, read it for yourself. What is he thinking of? I thought it was all decided. Why does he always want to be different? I don't know where he gets it from.'

'Don't you?' After twenty years of marriage, he still cannot predict her next move. He thinks back to the first time he saw her, the shooting party on her father's Scottish estate; she came into the room looking very glamorous, with bouncy blonde curls and sparkling blue eyes. They were married the next year. In the main, her spontaneity is very useful, but occasionally there are difficult consequences.

'Hmm. We must make sure that he comes out for the next holidays, so that we can have a good talk about it. At least he is going to have some guidance if he goes in the ATC.'

‘I suppose it will be an exciting thing to do, I am sure that with his personality and background, he will be good officer material. Neither the Fairweathers nor the Farquhars are run-of-the-mill types. I am sure he will make his mark.’

Istanbul

July 1969

Sir Charles Fairweather, sitting next to his wife, senses her excitement as the plane circles, preparing to land in Istanbul. The waterways are becoming distinct; the wide Bosphorus with ships in dock and in passage between the Black Sea and the Sea of Marmara.

Elspeth's eyes are on the minarets of mosques spiking up. Istanbul is somewhere she's always hankered to visit: the Blue Mosque, the Topkapi Palace and the Grand Bazaar. She spots the ferry crossing from Europe to Asia. She's on the edge of a final adventure. Even after all these years she has an upsurge of energy knowing there will be receptions, cocktail parties. Their friends, the Marrons, are stationed here too, entirely by coincidence, but a fitting end to Charles' years of service; they'd been in Kenya at his first posting.

As the plane lands, she touches Charles on the thigh and smiles.

Elspeth waits until the heat of the day has passed before visiting the bazaar. She's conspicuous, attired in a simple day-dress, her blonde hair shining. Next time she'll cover her head. She breathes in the pungent aroma of coffee, treading carefully to avoid a puddle of the black liquid next to the vendor's stall. Displays of huge onions in layers of concentric circles amongst bunches of fresh green herbs are impressive, but she doesn't need anything.

She moves into the spice market; the colours sing out, shades of vermilion, ochre and sienna. Tempting. Wandering down to the waterfront, she is enticed by the smell of fish cooking on charcoal barbecues. She smiles at the merchant and moves on. A ship's horn sounds, and she realises the ferry is leaving, clouds of black smoke wafting up into the air. She hopes that one day Charles will have time to join her in a journey to the Asian side of the Bosphorus.

July 1970

Charles frowns, instructions from on high. Somebody wants to make a name for himself. He pushes the documents away and leans back in his chair. He's running out of steam, should have retired at sixty as he'd intended. He purses his lips; wishes he hadn't given into the flattery. "You are our best man for the job. You can handle delicate situations." That, and Elspeth's enthusiasm for Istanbul, had been difficult to ignore. She's out on a solo expedition now; "making the most of it," she'd said when he'd pointed out the unrest. Would she use the gun if necessary?

Wishing they were back in Whistledon, he closes his eyes, sees the river, feels the water pushing against his waders, imagines the spinner glinting in the sunshine. He comes back to the room before a fish bites. He'll see this through and be back home for the spring. That will give him a summer before Angus needs help.

He huffs. "Oiling the wheels," that's the expression the PM used, apparently. Other countries are more in favour than GB, and their expertise in oil exploration on a par. A twinge of unease drops to the pit of his stomach. His reputation is at risk. No wonder the PM had mentioned the Queen's Birthday Honours.

He straightens the document on the table and stands. Time to arrange the room. Sweeteners have always been used. By a convenient coincidence, he has been given information that the expected consul wants to acquire a string of racehorses, something to turn to if his career ends abruptly. It's common knowledge that he is caught up in political flak. He takes a photograph of Angus, holding the reins of a splendid Arab horse with a glossy black coat, and places it carefully onto a side table. His son is looking cheerful and proud; he is sturdy with thick blond hair and an engaging smile. Angus will relish selecting a horse and it will be good practice for him. Another year and they will be in business themselves.

He stands viewing his work, listening. The ceiling fan is making a clicking sound on every turn. Slightly out of alignment. He must mention it to maintenance. Hearing the door open, he goes out to greet his tall guest. The face of the consul is arranged in an affable smile, too affable. He sees the brown eyes turn to the photograph on the side table.

'My son,' he says.

'That's a very fine horse.'

'I might be able to help.'

'That would be very kind of you. In return I have in mind an interesting ornament.'

Charles nods, picks up his pen and signs.

Elspeth puts her cheek to the pillow and sighs. When there was no official lunch, Charles used to take his siesta with her; a habit that started in Kenya. She'd taken pleasure in having him to herself and it had given them the energy to entertain in the evenings. Where is he now? Recently, at a reception, he'd paid undue attention to the very attractive wife of the consul he's negotiating with; Elspeth can't help thinking he might be with her. Did she give up her own career for this? If she had not married, she might still be in Edinburgh, a fashion reporter for the *Weekly Scotsman*? Or maybe she would have progressed to Paris. As a diplomat's wife she isn't allowed to work, and certainly not in areas where, heaven forbid, she might express opinions.

The bedroom door opens. 'Hello darling,' Charles glances down at her, 'you're having a long rest today. Don't forget that the Marrons will be here for tea. I've just been talking to the consul. He's going to send us an interesting ornament.'

Elspeth doesn't reply. She's wanted for some duties and glad of it really. It hurts, but she doesn't wish to be without him.

She brightens up as she dresses. The Marrons are good company and have invited them to visit their villa in Nice next year. Life is fine most of the time.

The shadows are lengthening across the lawn. Pierre Marron pushes his cup to one side and stretches. 'Time to go, I've still got some reading to catch up on.'

Charles smiles. 'I'm free this evening. Shall we stroll back with them and go on down to the waterfront?'

Elspeth nods, 'That would be good."

She stands looking down on the Bosphorus, the water shimmering with reflections of the sinking sun. A cargo ship is easing its way toward the shore, black against the golden sea.

The call-to-prayer is ringing out; Charles is reaching for her hand, wanting to walk on. She pushes him away. This is a memory to be treasured, remembered when she is back in Wales. She sweeps her eyes along the expanse of water, taking in the evening scene. She stiffens. She can see someone standing under a tree. He is staring at them, watching them. She holds her breath. Before she can say anything, his arm is raised. A shot rings out. A short, piercing cry comes from Charles. He crumples to the ground, blood running down his white shirt.

'Help! Help!' People are gathering. She drops to the ground beside Charles. Someone takes her hand. Others bend over Charles.

'We need an ambulance, but he's gone.' says a voice.

She trembles. Everything has changed.

4

Huw tips the whisky onto the ice. Scotch on the rocks. Can't beat it. He looks down on a sea of clouds, billowing white. He's glad to be away from the rain, and sharp winds. This investigation is intriguing, and the woman rather attractive. He's wearing his clerical collar; it usually gets him a little more space, possibly more attention from the airhostess in Business Class; this one has a curvaceous figure above some good legs. His eyes travel past her to the newspaper across the aisle. "ANOTHER SHOOTING. Second consul dead". Is there an anarchist going to extremes? He sips his whisky. Maybe an arms manufacturer is stirring the pot towards war, wanting to further production and profits. Reaching down, he pulls the file from his briefcase, checks he can't be overlooked, and re-reads the documents, studying the photographs.

In one, Lady Elspeth Fairweather is standing under palm trees wearing a vibrant blue evening gown, a quizzical expression on her face. In another, she's on horseback, accompanied by Sir Charles, and looking very relaxed and happy. In the last photo, of a tartan-dressed shooting party, presumably taken on the Scottish moors, she has a determined expression. Fascinating. He puts the folder away, looking forward to meeting her and to the beauty and excitement of Istanbul.

Emerging from the airport, the heat is stifling. Momentarily he regrets wearing the collar, but his driver easily identifies him and whisks him through streets bustling with tourists, to the air-conditioned hotel.

He showers, mentally preparing the letter he will write; he needs to couch it delicately to overcome her shock. The Foreign Office want to know more about the negotiations: who shot Charles and why? Did Charles confide in her?

He pours a beer from the fridge, takes a page of headed paper off the desk, and begins.

Sultanahmet Hotel, Istanbul,

Dear Lady Fairweather,

I offer you my deepest condolences on the death of your husband. Although I didn't know Charles personally, I have a great respect for his work in the diplomatic field.

As padre to the army, I have many years of experience in dealing with loss. The Foreign Office have asked me to help. You do not have to go through this alone.

Please contact me at the above address.

Yours sincerely,

Canon Huw Lloyd.

Now to stretch his legs and drop the letter in at the British Consulate.

Taking the letter out onto the sitting-room balcony, Elspeth shivers in the cool morning air. Can she refuse to meet the man? She doesn't want to talk to anyone. She looks down at the gardens; staff are arriving normally, walking past the cypress trees that line the official drive. Sprinklers are spraying the lawns. All is happening according to routine. There's no routine for her now. Is it all her fault? She wanted the excitement of Istanbul. She helped persuade Charles to take the posting. If he'd retired as originally planned, they'd be at home in the Hall. She wouldn't be a widow. She wouldn't have to go back to Wales without him. He's been her strength and support. Can she carry on living? Does she want to? She must, Angus and Katrina can't lose their mother as well as their father. Why didn't he tell her just how dangerous the post was? Or is it nothing to do with the unrest?

Combing his hair, Huw views himself in the full-length mirror. He's looking trim, his hair is still thick, dark brown with just a hint of silver. Pretty good for almost sixty. He straightens his grey tie and hesitates. Perhaps he should wear the dog collar. He needs to make the right impression, needs to win her confidence. Wrinkling his brow, he considers his reflection, decides the tie will be better. He gives the girl at Reception his room key, and smiling holds her gaze. She smiles back, fluttering her eye lids. He still has the touch.

Huw checks his watch. He is in good time. Entering, he recognises Lady Fairweather from the photographs. She's sitting in a green plush chair at the opposite side of the room. As he gets closer, he can see she is older now but still good looking. With outstretched arm, she motions him to sit. He takes the occasional chair and moves it nearer, gently placing his hand upon his own knee, leans slightly towards her. He feels a surge of pleasurable excitement. Take it slowly, Huw. Eye contact is the key. 'Good morning, my dear.'

She frowns. 'Good morning, Canon.'

'May I call you Elspeth?' He inclines his head. 'Please call me Huw.'

Her eyes will not meet his, they flick from side to side, up to the ceiling. She will be in shock of course; he leans towards her, slowly moving his hand across to her thigh, resting it gently. She does not flinch, brings her eyes to his face.

Elspeth lies awake in the darkness, a heavy feeling in her heart. The picture of Charles bleeding is haunting her mind. Part of her clings onto it and doesn't want to let it go, part wants to forget it and the rest desperately wants to go back a week when everything was normal. The canon said he'd come to help; he was very sure of himself. She'll ask him to pray with her. His brown eyes are quite piercing. How much does he know? She turns over, puts her face in the pillow. She won't tell him anything. Not even that Charles cheated on her. He was stupid, dallying about with that young wife; he knew that he was playing with fire. Other cultures are not as free and easy as ours; adultery is a serious business. Can it be called a crime of passion? She supposes it can. She can't bear the thought of life without him. Dreads another day to smile and pretend that she is ok. What has happened to the woman? Did *her* husband punish her too? He was obviously furious. It is no good lying here thinking dark thoughts, she needs to move. She will make herself a cup of tea.

Sipping the lightly scented tea, she reflects, the canon will be coming again this afternoon. Is she looking forward to it? Was he flirting with her yesterday? There is something about him that is intrusive. On the other hand, he did seem to understand. She needs something to do to stop herself thinking. She will go to the Grand Bazaar this morning; that is always fascinating.

Entering through the old stone-arch, Elspeth stops, her eye caught by a smiling young man holding up a flowered rug.

'See how beautiful it is.'

She puts out her hand and touches the soft blue carpet, admiring the intricate pattern.

'They are all hand-made by young women in the mountains. Come with me to my stall. I will give you a silk runner to show your friends.'

She shakes her head and steps to the side. This is too much; she shouldn't have come.

She moves to stand in front of a colourful array of spices. A voice says,

'Try one of my herbal teas. I have a love tea for you.'

'No, no thank you.'

It is too busy; she feels small and insignificant amongst the crowds, biting her lip to stop the tears. She turns to look at the next window, chock full of gold filigree. Intricate bracelets and necklaces, draped to entice. She stands, barely taking in the sight in front of her, until her eye is caught by an unexpected customer. Canon Lloyd. Huw is taking a wrapped purchase from the stallholder. She doesn't want to talk to him here, she swivels and gets lost in the throng, uncomfortable, almost embarrassed. There's something unsettling about him.

5

Leeds

1943

Simon, standing in the school morning assembly, swallows the lump in his throat and blinks back tears as the headmaster reads the last name on the list and puts it aside. He knew some of these Old Leonians, now killed in action or missing; they had been prefects and house captains in the years above him. He can't imagine what it must have been like for them.

What a waste of life. When will the war end? His stomach lurches at the thought that one day, his name might be read out.

'Let us pray.' The words filter into his consciousness. Simon bows his head as they all recite the Lord's Prayer.

The fog is creeping in as evening falls. Simon, leaving the after-school session of the army cadets, takes his cycle from the rack behind the gym and pushes it across the playground to the road. He wants to get home before it is completely dark. He knows the way well enough in the twilight, but distances seem to change in the fog, especially without any lights around. His satchel is heavy on his back, an evening of homework to be done, and piano practice, stretches before him.

Opening the front door, he can hear his mother softly singing, “Lead Kindly Light”, as she sets the table for tea. Hanging his coat on the hall stand, he makes his mind up, he will talk to her now. He walks over to the fireplace in the dining room, stands in front of the blazing coals. It is comforting. He turns,

‘Mum, what chance is there that Dad will agree to me going to Cambridge after the war?’

She raises her eyebrows. ‘What do you want to go there for? All highfalutin airs and graces.’

‘Can you at least help persuade him to let me stay on at school; I shall need Highers.’

‘I’m not sure about that. He was only saying last night that he believes there will be a place going in the weighing department in July. He thinks it's time you settle down to reality. Never mind fantasising about becoming a music scholar.’

‘The careers tutor suggests I read Classics at Cambridge.’

‘Is that what you want to do?’

‘I told him theology. It’s not my first choice, but you and Dad both said going to the Manchester College of Music wasn’t an option.’

‘Well, you can’t make much of a living playing music. What about doing accountancy?’

Simon looks up to the ceiling. 'Oh, help me, God. You're as bad as he is. I am not joining the family firm.'

'I am not saying you should. Although that would make your father happy.'

'It's *my* life we're talking about. Not his.'

'What about being a solicitor, or an architect? They get paid well.'

'It's not all about money. I think I would make a good vicar.'

'That's a surprise, perhaps you might! They don't earn much, so you will be happy about that.'

Simon rolls his eyes. 'Old Wilko thinks I should try for Cambridge to read Classics. I told him I want to take Music, Greek and History, next year.'

Putting the last knife in place, she hurries to the kitchen.

He raises his voice. 'He said Latin, Greek and History would be better.' He follows her. 'Old Wilko was in the First World War, killed men, watched his friends die. "You kill them, or they kill you", he said. He told us all the gory details. I know Father expects me to do my duty and that Britain needs defending, but I don't want to kill innocent people or fellows who are no more in favour of war than I am.'

'You could become a conscientious objector'.

He scowls. 'That seems cowardly.'

'I think it takes a lot of courage to be one of those. Don't you know they were shot by their own officers?'

He shakes his head. 'Why am I not surprised?'

Simon is still in two minds about his future as he pumps up his tyres ready to cycle to his Saturday stint at Aunt Vi's shop. He gives the second tyre a final squeeze, then satisfied with his efforts, he screws on the hub cap, puts his pump back onto the frame and swings his leg over the saddle.

As he pedals along the leafy roads near his home, he looks forward to talking to her. She is far more outgoing than Mother, she has to be, her husband was killed in a bombing raid. And as she says, "she needs to keep the money rolling in". Simon is happy to receive payment for his job. It's enough cash to take Abbi to the cinema. Of all the girls that come into the shop, she's the only one he fancies. He's going to ask her out when he sees her next, if he can fit her in between this job, homework, piano practice and choir.

Simon wheels his bike past the chemists and the beer-off, relishing the smell of battered fish from the next-door chip shop, before pushing his bike around to the back of Auntie Vi's sweets and tobacconists'. He props it up against the wall and knocks on the door.

Auntie Vi is quick to open it. 'Come in, lad.' she welcomes, screwing the lid off a large empty jar.

He hurries to help with the consignment from his father's factory, straddling the cardboard boxes strewn across the stockroom floor, breathing in the mixture of sweet smells. He slits the tape on a box, revealing bright yellow sherbets; his eyes light up.

Watching him she says, 'Go on then, just one, mind.'

He takes one, pops it into his mouth sucking hard, waits for the fizz. A grin encompasses his face.

'You're a right big kid!'

The grin disappears; he sighs and pulls a face. 'Dad's being an awful bore. I can't convince him that I don't want to go into the business.'

She rests the half-full jar of humbugs on her lap. He feels her eyes looking at him intently.

'You've got a lot about you. You're a clever lad. Don't waste it.'

'I'm thinking of going into the Church.'

Her eyes widen. 'That's a big decision.'

'Somebody needs to speak up for peace, love and understanding.' He scoops up the lemon sherbets, filling a jar and screwing on the top.

Cambridge

1946

Simon needs to escape. His first term at university is proving a bit of a trial. His fellow students seem to take themselves too seriously, need to lighten up. He feels a bit of a fish out of water; there are few northerners, and his West Yorkshire accent seems to set him apart. He would like to meet some girls but there seems little opportunity, apart from the local dances; there's a preponderance of males at the colleges and he hasn't found anyone on his wavelength yet. He closes his shared bedroom door firmly and strides out into the town.

He joins the queue at the Arts Picture House. This week's film is said to be extremely funny; he is ready to have some light relief. He pushes his hands deep into his pockets to keep them warm and quietly stamps his feet. The queue is moving very slowly; despite the stamping he's beginning to lose the feeling in his toes. The young women in front of him start jumping up and down, giggling. They are obviously all good friends; he is enjoying watching them. He tries not to stare but one of them is extremely attractive. She has a smile which seems to spread right across her pink round face and a laugh that seems–to run up and down in trills. She sounds to have a Welsh accent; he cocks his ear but can't make out the words. She waves her arms about energetically to make her points; it's obviously a good story because they all become convulsed in laughter. He wishes that he'd got friends who would enjoy this film.

He follows the uniformed usherette as she shines her torch to show him to the row with the vacant place. He squeezes past a group of cackling, elderly women, before sinking into the seat. The neighbouring woman nudges him. 'You've missed some good stuff. You must stay to see the beginning.'

He settles down. The antics on the screen are slapstick, amusing. No need to think. He watches as the group is escorted to seats a few rows forward from him. There is a buzz as they make their way along the row. Their animation fits in well with the film and soon he can hear that distinctive laugh ringing out. He decides to stay to watch from the beginning, as recommended by his neighbour.

The rows in front of him are emptying. He's tempted to follow the girl but wouldn't know what to say. He sits tight. He wonders what she's doing in Cambridge. She seems very down to earth, not like most of the people he's come across. It's a rarefied atmosphere, even though the war has made changes to the type of students the colleges are accepting.

Afterwards he calls into the Copper Kettle for a cup of tea and a toasted teacake. The grey-haired waitress remembers him from a previous visit and quietly gives him some extra sugar lumps. He smiles his thanks.

He has no lectures on Monday morning. Making his way to the library, he passes the College Information Board. He notices that a madrigal group meets in a church hall, every Tuesday at 7p.m. He perks up; he sang with the school Madrigal Society. He will go and hopefully meet some like-minded people. There might be some interesting girls.

Anxious not to arrive with all eyes looking at him, he sets off early and gets there as the vicar is about to unlock the Hall door. The clergyman is delighted when he finds that Simon is studying theology and stays talking until a few members come drifting in. They are not all students and vary in age from school pupil to middle-aged men and women. Simon is pleased that there are several from the women's college, all singing with great concentration.

He catches the eye of a dark-haired soprano; she looks away immediately, but at the tea break he wanders across to where she is standing with another girl. They chat until the choir master calls them to order again.

On his way back, he calls into the Copper Kettle. She's there, the attractive girl with the laugh, but she is with a man. They exchange smiles as he makes his way to a table. He notices how his heart is beating a little faster, he wants to know if she has a boyfriend. She's not there when he leaves. He determines to put her out of his mind and, next week, thinking that a shared interest in music could form the basis of a good relationship, he asks the soprano out for a drink. The evening goes quite well; she enthuses about the Sacred Art exhibition at the Fitzwilliam Museum; he thinks he might go and see for himself. When he begins to talk about the rebuilding of Britain, he notices her eyes become glazed. They part without making another date.

Back in his room, he kneels. God, please show me the way forward. I would like a girlfriend, if that is your will.

The next day, Simon sets off for the Fitzwilliam Museum, his rucksack on his back. He wonders how useful an exhibition of sacred art can be to his theology course; Simon has never really been bothered about art. He finds the huge paintings on the ceilings of Roman Catholic churches a little intimidating. "God is watching you". He appreciates the skill of painters, but he's a photographer, likes to capture landscapes, seascapes, flora and fauna, and make prints from them. However, the woman was so keen that he visit the exhibition, he feels he needs to give it his attention, especially as the theme is Sacred Art.

There are a few people already inside, standing in front of the exhibits. He wonders what has brought them here. Are they artists or interested in religion and its history? He supposes it will give him clues as to how Christianity has developed over the years. The history of its arrival in Europe. All messages are changed with the messenger's input. Even the Bible's meaning was changed in translation. Is his faith strong enough? His path is clear. He needs to study all aspects if he is to help people. He leaves his rucksack with the attendant by the door, taking out his notebook and pencil, ready to jot down anything that seems relevant to his study. The development of Christianity in Britain. Sacred Art might be the subject of an essay, he could use it to illustrate the ways people were taught before they could read.

Moving slowly from picture to picture, Simon is impressed by the way one artist creates the illusion of light shining on the subject. He is busy scribbling down notes when he feels a tap on his shoulder.

'These are particularly brilliant don't you think?' says a Welsh voice.

He turns to answer and is excited to see it's the girl from the cafe and the queue. He feels a blush creeping up his body until he knows his face must be crimson.

'I'm sorry if I made you jump. I wonder if you are on the same course as I am? I haven't seen you in lectures.'

'No, no. We haven't got any women.'

'What are you doing then? When I saw you making notes, I thought you must be on the History of Art like me.' She holds out a sketch that she has just started.

'That's very good', he says. 'I don't find drawing easy.'

She laughs. 'Neither do I, but I enjoy trying. I'm fascinated by the ways other people make pictures. So, what are you doing?'

'Theology.'

'Oh. That must be quite daunting, but very interesting. Do you have to know the Bible inside out?'

Simon laughs. 'I think that would be impossible. I've only just begun. I'm thinking about the history of Christianity at the moment.' He drops his voice, suddenly aware that they are becoming loud and are receiving disapproving looks from a thin-lipped woman in a navy gaberdine coat. 'I think we ought to carry on this conversation somewhere else'.

She nods. Her bright eyes meet his. He closes his notebook and buzzing with excitement, leads the way out of the gallery.

He pauses to collect his rucksack, stuffing his notebook back in, he says 'I'm Simon. Shall we go to the Copper Kettle for a coffee?'

'I'm Claire. That sounds a lovely idea.'

Doncaster

1951

Leaving the small, terraced house, Simon shuts the front door as quietly as he can. The step is bright donkey stone white; the grieving widow is keeping herself occupied with her usual chores. It is less than a week since the funeral. The prayers he said seemed to help, but it is difficult to tell, particularly with the family not being regular churchgoers. He expects he will get better at the job with experience.

It's good that he hasn't far to walk, his ears are cold; he holds his scarf to his throat with one hand and tucks his books firmly under his arm with the other. He doesn't envy the widow and her children having to use their outside toilet in this weather, and it will be even worse if it snows.

With a stab of guilt, he unlatches his garden gate, walks up the path to the open porch, with its sparkling stained-glass windows. He has always had a good-sized, comfortable home and never been short of money. The inequalities in society are disturbing.

In the hall, he can smell a cake baking. Claire, carrying Dinah, kisses him on the cheek. 'How did it go?'

'As well as I could expect.' He puts his books down, takes off his coat, and holds up his arms.

'I've just fed her. She could probably do with winding.'

He pulls Dinah into his shoulder and begins gently rubbing her back. 'I should have gone into politics instead of the church. I'd be able to say what I really think, not have to feed platitudes to a congregation that goes through the motions and doesn't question the status quo.'

Claire laughs and pulls a face. 'I don't think I would like to be a politician's wife. Anyway, your sermons are always interesting.'

He is not sure about that.

In the dining room, the clock on the mantelpiece strikes twelve. Claire, spreading a starched white cloth on to the table, hurries to the bottom of the stairs. 'Simon, you'll be late for the train if you don't go in five minutes.'

Simon, pulling on his jacket, comes running downstairs. 'I know, I was just making sure that her bedroom is ready.'

'Of course it is. I saw to that first thing. I hope she will be ok. It's lovely that she wants to come for a few nights.'

'You'll like her when you get to know her properly.'

'I'm intrigued. I've never met anyone who talks to people who've passed away. I'm a little apprehensive.'

'There's no need to be. She won't mention it unless you ask her about it.'

The station is busy. Simon weaves his way through people hurrying along the tiled underground tunnel. He runs up the steps to the platform, spotting Aunt Violet, just in time to take her suitcase before she climbs down from the carriage.

The massive black steam engine fires up, hissing, ready to move on.

She straightens her hat and pulls her musquash fur coat around her, fastens the toggles.

'Mind what you do with that. It's got a cake in it.'

He sets the case on the ground, with exaggerated care, gives her a peck on the cheek.

She, clutching a large crocodile skin handbag in one hand, wraps her free arm around him. 'I can't wait to meet the new arrival. Have you chosen her name yet?'

Simon beams proudly, 'Dinah. We finally decided.'

Violet smiles. 'Not following the family tradition, then. I thought she might be Rose.'

He picks up her luggage again and shakes his head, leads her down the stairs and out of the station to his Morris Minor. 'Here we are.' He puts the case in the boot, as Violet edges herself into the small car.

'Sorry, it's a bit cramped. Father bought it, so we could visit him.' He feels slightly guilty that he hasn't been lately, only once since mother died.

'How do you like living in Doncaster?'

'It's ok. There's a big, busy market. Claire shops there at least once a week.'

'I expect you need good, cheap food on a curate's stipend.'

'How's the shop?'

'Doing very well. It should pick up even more when rationing ends. Your father looks after me, but I've got a friend minding it over Christmas.'

Parking on the road, Simon leads the way, mindful of the cake in the case he is carrying. Two cakes in one day. Things are going well.

'Can I help?' Violet is already putting on her "pinny", wrapping the tape around her and tying it at the front.

'Auntie, you've not been here two minutes. Don't you want to relax? Besides, I've only the gravy to make, then we can eat.'

She smiles. 'That daughter of yours is a bonny lass.'

Claire raises her eyebrows. 'Wait till she wakes up and see what you think then. She's already got a mind of her own.'

Whistledon on Wye

1969

Simon glimpses St Peters hiding behind an ancient yew tree. With increasing anticipation, he strides up the slope, pushes open the wooden gate, and going through, meticulously closes it before walking between the well-tended graves towards the tubs of bright orange nasturtiums that frame the entrance porch. He glances at the information on the noticeboard. He's looking forward to putting faces to the names.

Pushing open the heavy oak door, his gaze takes in rows of dark wooden pews either side of the aisle. He pauses at the front pew; heavily carved pineapples boast the wealth of the Fairweather family. No-one else has their own pew. A rush of anger surges as he realises the amount of wealth this family has been privileged to have for centuries. Ill-gotten gains.

On the right, below the pulpit, stands an impressive arrangement of white dahlias. He must meet the lady responsible and thank her. A grand piano sits next to the flowers. The bishop had warned him that the organ was to be taken away for refurbishment; he might have known the Fairweathers wouldn't replace it with the usual tin-pot instrument. Simon has never played anything other than a standard upright. He walks across and caresses the keys. The notes ring out clear and true. He props open the lid and plays a scale. The bell-like sound echoes around the church; the acoustics are good. It will be wonderful to hear Welsh voices singing.

His eyes travel up to a plaque on the opposite wall.

"In loving memory of LT. CDR. HENRY MORGAN FAIRWEATHER R.N. 1910-1943"

They suffered too. Who didn't?

The meeting with the churchwardens went well. Perhaps he should have told them that Dinah is a Pagan. No, it would have been silly. She's young. Not many young people come to church these days. He's beginning to understand her thinking. She says it's the same God but without all the piety. If only people weren't so keen to make religion into a battleground. God is love. How many people really think that? Most seem to see God as a retributive force, on their side if they keep the Church's rules. Some people still believe the earth is flat and God sits upon a cloud above them. Simon will reach out to all the villagers.

Making his way to the gleaming old carved oak pulpit, he runs his hand along the rail, feels the patina of years. He climbs the stairs slowly, turns to face the empty pews, imagines faces gazing up at him. What is he going to preach? He isn't positive that he can explain his thoughts. The recent landings on the moon are a paradigm shift. Some say it's all a great hoax.

In the rectory, Claire and Dinah have Culpepper's Herbal open on the table in front of them.

'Your dad has offered to dig over the garden and set some potatoes.'

'Good for him. I'll give a hand when I'm here.'

Claire raises her eyebrows.

'Why are you looking at me like that?'

'I'm just surprised. I didn't realise you liked gardening.'

'Come on, Mum, allow me to change. Please.'

'Of course. It will be lovely to have your help.'

'Actually, there are a few herbs that would be useful for the group.'

'Make a list and I'll sow the seeds in the greenhouse, and you can plant them out in April or May. That's if you have time.'

Dinah grabs a piece of paper and starts listing plants.

Claire glances at the clock. 'Shall we find him, have another look at the church?'

Simon steps down from the pulpit as Claire and Dinah come in. 'I'm preparing for the challenge.'

'Keep praying about it. All will become clear.' Claire, walking towards the altar, stops abruptly, stands, her eye caught by a stained-glass window, vivid with colour in the afternoon sun. Shades of blue zing out as fishermen haul in a net laden with fish.

'There are some treasures here! I suppose the craftsmen wanted to make sure of their places in Heaven.'

'I expect Morgan Fairweather had that in mind for himself, too.' Simon makes his way around the pews to stand beside her.

'Is there a craftsman's mark?' Dinah is on her toes, trying to scrutinise the bottom of the panel.

Claire shakes her head. 'Not that I can see.'

'Come on, I'll show you the font.' Simon leads them towards the main door.

'Wow! I've never seen anything like this before.' Dinah points to a tall carved wooden cover on the font. 'Those carvings look extremely unusual, I wonder how old it is,'

Simon's eyes light up. 'I'm told there are only a few in the country.' He pulls open the heavy door and stands back while the women go through.

6

Whistledon on Wye

1970

Elspeth picks up the brightly drawn card inviting her to the village school's harvest festival. A beaming farmer sits upon a combine harvester; she turns the card over. When does it start? She has time to walk down to the church if she goes now. She remembers Charles insisting they went two years ago; he would want her to do so now. It is her last duty before going to Auchdair. She dashes on some lipstick and sets off. The walk will do her good.

Simon stands in the nave, eyes upon the church door, ready to escort Lady Fairweather to her pew. The church is full. Polished red apples, bright tomatoes, a large cabbage, big onions and scrubbed carrots are held in small hands, awaiting placement on the trestle table near the altar, already arrayed with various types of bread. Sheaves of corn fringe the steps to the pulpit.

He hopes his sermon will catch the children's interest. In other years he has said, "harvest is a time for rejoicing"; that would be heartless in the presence of Lady Fairweather. But where is she? He looks at his watch, gives the nod to the verger to close the door and makes his way to the front of the church.

It is no good, she can't face the graveyard. Walking away from the path, into the orchard, tears splash down Elspeth's cheeks. Enclosing a ripe pippin in her fingers, she gently plucks it from the tree, the first apple Charles ever offered her.

She stands amidst the cider apples that have already fallen, her attention on a large one, its scarlet skin glistening against the fading grass. She picks it up, flinches as a wasp flies out of the brown soggy underside. Beautiful on top but rotten underneath. Sighing, she closes her eyes against the buzzing wasp; keep still, pretend to be invisible, maybe it will all go away. From somewhere deep inside a voice whispers, "you know that's impossible." The sooner she leaves here the better. At Auchdair, she won't be constantly reminded of Charles. The buzzing stops, the wasp has gone. She walks briskly back to the Hall.

7

Auchdair

31st October 1970

Elspeth wakes with a start. Where is she? Slowly the room takes shape around her, the worn dressing table and wardrobe, the large window looking towards the hills. She swings her legs out of bed and goes to look out. It is a beautiful morning; there is a clear view over the valley; she can see red deer grazing. Thank goodness she has escaped from Whistledon, and that haunting image. It is a relief to be here. Last night, Robbie suggested that she gives their pony, Nelly, some exercise. She will do that soon.

Her thoughts are broken by a knock on the door and Robbie's voice,

'A cup of tea for you, sister.'

She gets back into bed. Pulls the bedclothes up around her ears. She has forgotten how icy it can be. How much colder than Wales, the days are shorter, the sun lower.

Robbie comes in, all smiles, 'I've added a wee dram to warm you up.' He gives her a broad grin as he puts the cup down on the bedside table. 'I hope you slept well. Breakfast is in half-an-hour. Angus wants to get off.'

'I know.' He was quite short with me yesterday. 'He needs to get back for his meeting with the architect.' She takes a deep breath. 'I've interrupted his work, but it's good to be here. Thank you, Robbie, I won't be long.'

He pauses at the door,' I've been wondering; would you like to rent one of the cottages? You could make it your permanent home.'

Her eyes widen. 'That's a tempting idea.' A small cottage will be warm. 'Can I think about it?'

'Of course, take as long as you like.'

Elspeth watching Angus' car disappear down the road, turns to Robbie, 'Is it ok if I go to the stables now?'

'I thought you might like to come into the village with me. I need to go to the post office with this flyer about the ceilidh we're going to have. I can show you the new hall.'

He strides out, Elspeth hurries to keep up with him.

He grins. 'It's good to see you've still got a good pace in you.'

'You taught me the hard way.'

'Hard for me, you mean. I was the one that got the rollicking for your tardy appearance at dinner.'

'I was only seven. If it hadn't been for the doctor passing in his car, I might never have got home.'

Robbie roars with laughter. 'You were older than that. How was I to know you had no sense of direction?'

As they pass the church she smiles, remembering her wedding day and looks up at the heather moor, where she took Charles shooting. Tears come to her eyes, she married a good man, they enjoyed each other's company. She can smell smoke rising from a garden bonfire.

'Here we are.' Robbie takes some keys out of his pocket. 'The new village hall. What do you think? It's a joint venture between the estate and the church. It's good to keep the workers happy. I'll show you around.'

Elspeth looks at the long room with its new light wood floor. She does a little jig, 'My, this is impressive. A lot better than the dark dusty one I remember, but we had some good times. Mother used to raise her eyebrows.'

Robbie raises his, 'Yes, she wondered what prank you would dream up next.'

'It was all good harmless fun. I hope you've got something lined up for Hogmanay.'

'Yes, indeed! A ceilidh with some cracking pipers. Come on, I'm supposed to be working.'

'Lady Fairweather, I'm so pleased to meet you. Customers often talk about the times they had when you were here.' The post-mistress glances at Robbie. 'No offence Lord Farquhar.'

'None taken. You can tell people to get their dancing shoes out.' He hands her a poster advertising the ceilidh. 'Would you be good enough to display this?'

'Och, what excitement. You'll be coming, Lady Fairweather? I'm sure it will brighten us all up.'

Elspeth nods. 'It's lovely to meet you. I can see the post office is in good hands.'

'The Highlands is a wonderful place to stay. I'm from Edinburgh but I love the wild beauty here. I've seen eagles, magnificent, but I do worry about the lambs in the valley.'

Elspeth turns and looks around the well-stocked village store, selects a knitting pattern and some wool for a jumper. She will need something to do in the long evenings; she won't be able to dance reels to the bagpipes every night.

It is late afternoon before Elspeth can ride Nelly. Giving her a hand up into the saddle Robbie says, 'You'd best not be out too long; the light will soon be fading.'

'I'll just ride to the mill.' Elspeth pats Nelly on the neck, the pony's hooves clip-clopping on the concrete. Away from the shelter of the buildings, the cold air strikes her face, and Elspeth is glad to have the pony's warm body beneath her. Fallen leaves are covering the path, damp with early-afternoon rain. October is nearly over.

When they reach the turf, Nelly canters, almost with a spring in her step, as though she is pleased to have a change of scene. As the terrain becomes steeper the pony slows, places her hooves more deliberately. They reach the level grassy surface and gallop onwards, enjoying the outing. After another ten minutes, when the loch is not yet in view, Elspeth has a heavy feeling in her chest; is she lost? It's a long time since she has been here. Has she taken the wrong path? She pulls Nelly to a halt, looks around. There is no-one in sight. She sits tall, everything appears different. Nelly is trembling. Feeling her tension, Elspeth strokes the sweaty neck. Urging her to walk on along the stony track, Elspeth relaxes as she recognises a wide valley with few trees, knows that it leads to the loch and the derelict mill.

The building is more dilapidated than she expected; ferns are sprouting through the paddles in the old wooden waterwheel, young trees are pushing up out of the broken walls, stones are strewn across the path. She dismounts and leads Nelly carefully through the debris.

Two carrion crows land nearby, beady eyes gaze at her; they stalk across the grass, curved beaks tug at a sheep's carcass. Shudders run up her spine. She opens her flask, takes a quick drink. Nelly snorts, rearing. Elspeth grabs the reins, pulls the pony's head down, stroking her. Elspeth's chest is tight, her breathing ragged. Why has she come here? Leaning against a wall she steadies herself; she needs to go. Remounting, she sets off back down the narrow winding path. Nelly is resistant. Stops. She gently urges her on. The little pony won't budge. Elspeth waiting for her to move, sits passively looking at the waterwheel. She tenses; a tall hazy figure is staring at her. She blinks, looks again. It has gone. She can hear water rushing out of the loch, nothing else, then wings beating as the crows rise skyward and disappear. Nelly moves quickly. Elspeth lurches forward, clinging onto the coarse hair of the mane, uprights herself. Rain clouds are looming. She urges the pony forward, glad of her company.

At last, the castle is visible through the gathering dusk. Her breathing eases. Did she imagine the apparition? Nelly trots briskly, seems pleased to be nearing home.

8

Whistledon on Wye

5 November 1970

The estate manager stubs out his cigarette before stuffing the papers into his briefcase.

Angus leans back in his chair and looks at the clock. That was a long session, but all seems to be running smoothly. A loud bang outside reminds him that it is Bonfire Night.

As he shows his visitor out, fireworks light up the sky, rockets whoosh up into the darkness, exploding, scattering down myriads of coloured stars. A visit to the village bonfire might be fun, light relief after all the detailed discussion he's just had.

Nearing the lodge at the bottom of the drive, excited voices, shouts and laughter carry across the distance.

By the time he arrives, the pile of logs accumulated over the past few weeks is well alight, sending sparks flying. The remnants of the stuffed sweater and trousers, that made-up the Guy, are twisting and falling into the flames. Smells of roasting chestnuts and jacket potatoes are enticing but he bypasses those stalls. He can see toffee apples being sold by the rector's wife. Making his way there, he dodges sparklers being waved by children drawing patterns in the air.

'It's good to see you, Sir Angus.' Claire wraps paper around the stick of a toffee-apple and hands it to him.

'Did you make these yourself?'

'I did. Bonfire night wouldn't be the same without them.'

He hands her a shilling and moves towards the fire, stands licking the toffee, biting the apple, feeling the warmth on his face.

Over the far side of the field, three men are lighting Catherine wheels., the rector is one of them. They move back as the spiralling lights cause oohs and aahs from the little crowd. Angus recognises one or two people from the farms. He nods to them, and they nod back. He is not in the mood for talking. He has an uncomfortable feeling that he is not socialising. Mother would be chatting to them, asking about their families. She would not be worrying about remembering names.

He leaves early, needing to check on the horses. This is the first real test of Hebrew's temperament since the fall at York. Rodney was right to suggest he bought the injured horse at a bargain price; the ligament is healing well. At this thought, he quickens his step.

Arriving at the Hall, he takes a lantern and strides across to the stable block. Unlocking the door, talking quietly and calmly, he approaches Hebrew. The horse, moving his head in recognition, seems unperturbed.

'Jolly good, old chap, I think you will do.' Ezra stirs; he pats him. He moves on to Nancy's stall, strokes her nose; she leans into him. 'Good night, old girl.'

Satisfied, Angus relocks the door and makes his way back to the house.

In the lounge, he picks up a bottle of Glenfiddich from the top of the cocktail cabinet and settles down into an armchair.

Angus sits up abruptly, as the clang of his alarm breaks into his deep sleep. He pulls the curtains back to reveal a dark cloudy sky. Sounds of Clive stoking the boiler rise from the outhouse; the ancient iron radiators creak and clang as the hot water begins to flow. Pulling on his work-clothes, Angus treads slowly down the stairs to the kitchen; he needs a cup of tea.

Gertrude gives a knowing nod as she passes him the strong sweet liquid. He nods back and grimaces.

Trudging across to the stable yard, Angus shivers inside his bomber jacket. The damp air clings, seeping into his bones as he moves his head, gently trying to lose the effects of last night's whisky. The smoke from fireworks is still hanging in the air.

He saddles Hebrew and canters to the river, eerily still in the morning light. A heron is standing in the water. He pulls the horse to a halt, watching as the bird impales a fish, tosses it up in the air and swallows.

Angus hates this weather and tries to shake off the gloom that's descended on him. His future is here, the beginning of a big project, one that Pa was going to be part of. He wonders how Katrina is coping. She'll be busy with the children and James. He needs someone to use as a sounding-board. He thinks back to his time in the RAF, there was always someone handy to discuss problems. Toby was good. He pats Hebrew's neck. Rodney won't be coming until next year. Perhaps he ought to get away while he still can. Toby hasn't found a settled job; he might keep him company; they could take a cruise.

9

Upper Whistledon Hall

24 December 1970

Angus picks up a mince pie from the table.; takes a bite. Gertrude has done a good job with the brandy in the filling. Let the festivities begin.

The Christmas tree in the corner stands well. Freshly cut and brought in by Clive and the old gardener, Bill Bates. Angus breathes in the smell of fresh pine. You can't beat a tree when it's newly cut. He removes some sparkling gold tinsel and places it higher up; Gertrude has an exuberant touch when it comes to decoration. He turns and takes the sherry bottle, fills a glass for himself. He can hear footsteps, recognises the rector's deep Yorkshire voice booming out, his wife's musical laugh chiming in. Clive is obviously on form tonight. There is a soft giggle, the daughter must be home for Christmas, he readies himself with a smile. Ma would be pleased with the effort he is making.

The Shorthouse family troop in, the rector explaining that they must leave in time to prepare for the late service. The daughter looks well. Oxford must be suiting her. She has developed a much more confident smile. He holds out a plate of sausage rolls. She takes one, bites into it, looking directly into his eyes as she does. She has certainly blossomed. Is she flirting with him? The doorbell is ringing again.

He nods as the farm manager, looking shiny clean in an embroidered waistcoat, comes in with his wife.

'Good to see you. Help yourselves.' Where is Clive? Angus looks around the noisy conservatory for the handyman; the village butcher is proudly touting the plate of pigs-in-blankets to Bill Bates. Gertrude, her best flowered dress covering her well corseted body, is offering vol au vents. Clive joins the party, picks up the wine and tops up glasses. Angus relaxes.

Opening a bottle of gin, he takes two glasses and puts a good measure into each, topping them up with ice and orange juice, then makes a beeline for Dinah. 'Can I interest you in a gin and orange?'

She smiles and, nodding her thanks, takes the glass. He seats himself next to her.

'Well then, how is life in Oxford?'

'It's great, thank you. I've become good friends with some fascinating people. They are Pagans. My course is good too.'

'What are you taking?'

'Archaeology and Ancient History. I get on well with my tutor. He's American and passionate about archaeology.'

'I'm pleased you're having fun. I don't think I'd have the patience to scrape about in the dirt looking for artefacts.'

'We've just been on an amazing weekend, unearthing an Anglo-Saxon village, but we're all different. That looked a lovely horse you were on yesterday. I admire the way you ride.'

Their eyes meet. Hers are twinkling. She *is* flirting with him. 'That's Hebrew, my first racehorse. I'm going to buy more next year.' He points to her empty glass. 'Can I get you another?'

She nods.

He strides to where Clive Robinson is pouring the drinks. 'It seems to be going well.'

'I think we'll need more red wine,' he says, topping up the gin with orange.

'That's fine, get some.' Angus heads back to Dinah, who is humming along to the sound of Jingle Bells coming from the record player.

Simon stands, walks across the room, 'It's time to go, I'm sorry it's been a brief visit, but duty calls.'

'I'll see you in the morning.'

Angus looks at Dinah. She's sticking up for herself. 'I'll make sure she gets home safely.'

'Thank you, Sir Angus.' Claire smiles. 'It's been a lovely evening.'

Simon and Claire's departure prompts Angus to nod to Gertrude and Clive. The housekeeper has expressed a wish to leave the party early, to go to the candle-lit service, insisting that there is something magical about the event.

The farmers and Bill are having a noisy discussion about the likelihood of a frost soon.

Angus turns to Dinah. 'Would you mind giving me a hand to fetch some more ice?'

Leading the way towards the kitchen, he becomes aware that she has stopped and is kneeling, her fingers tracing the pattern on the glazed, brown tiles. He bends, pulls her towards him, puts his hand around her waist; she rests in towards his shoulder. He leans against the wall; she snuggles close; he puts his other arm around her. 'Come here.' His mouth is on hers, his hands searching her body. She responds. He leads her away from the kitchen, through a dark passageway and into a small room with a sofa. He senses her uncertainty.

'It's ok, we won't be disturbed.'

10

January 1971

Lisbon

Dear Mother,

I thought that I had better tell you that I shall be away for five months. Toby and I embarked at Southampton on Thursday. We are here, in Lisbon, for another night whilst more passengers join us on the cruise. We've got an excellent cabin with a balcony and extremely helpful staff. It seems to be a good choice of ship. Tomorrow, we leave for Cape Town and should be in Sydney by the beginning of March. It is good to be missing the dreary winter months.

I hope that you are well and coping with the weather in the Highlands.

Love,

Angus

11

Whistledon on Wye

Bill Bates bites the hot sausage sandwich Gertrude has made for his breakfast; it's just what he needs on this cold February day. He looks up. Was that a drop of rain? He doesn't want a soaking. He hurries back down the drive to the Lodge. A large van is pulling up outside. The driver leans out of the window.

'Hello mate, what do you want doing with this? It's a heavy one.'

Bill scratches his head. 'Who is it for?'

'Sir Charles Fairweather.'

'He's not here anymore. He's dead. Shot, you know.'

'Well, I'm not taking it back. Deer stalking, was he?'

Bill shakes his head. 'It's Sir Angus now, and he's on a fancy cruise. Left me in charge. I've got a shed you can put it in. It'll be all right there.'

'Where is this shed then? Hop in, you're getting wet. Show me the way. You can help me unload.'

In the paddock, Hebrew and the two Welsh cobs, trot to the fence, looking curiously at the vehicle and the two men heaving a huge crate out of it.

‘I see what you mean.’

‘Here, give me a hand to steady it.’

Rain dripping from his hair, Bill glares at him and puts his hand on the crate as the driver pushes the trolley to the shed and yanks open the door. Together they ease the load inside.

The van gone, Bill stands looking at the crate, then carefully prises off one of the top slats, peels away some of the wrapping. He can see what looks like marble, smooth and shiny. Something for the garden. It will be fine here until Angus gets back.

12

Whistledon on Wye

April 1971

Claire puts the sheets onto Dinah's bed, wrestles with the duvet. She sings a little song to herself, glad that her daughter is coming for a few days. Simon has gone to the station to meet her. Claire wanted to go with him, but a member of the flower rota had called to discuss the Easter arrangement and Claire felt it rude to turn her away, especially as the woman was new to the village and seemed a little shy.

The Oxford train pulls slowly into the short platform at Whistledon Halt. Dinah hops down, rucksack on her back.

'Welcome home.'

She smiles. 'Lovely to be here. How's it going? Are the parishioners still turning up to services?'

'So far so good. But I would like more young people to attend.'

'If they are anything like me, they'll think it's all too formal, too much pomposity.'

Claire, hearing the car pull into the drive, dashes downstairs and out of the door, Cilla and Spike bounding after her, as Dinah is emerging from the passenger seat. They rush towards her, barking, tails wagging furiously. Dinah bends, pats them, a hand on each, straightens as her mother reaches out.

Clare hugs her. My, you're looking well. Oxford seems to be suiting you. You are positively glowing, and I think you've put a bit of weight on.'

Simon, following Dinah, nods. 'She certainly does look good.'

'I've been eating well. One of my friends is going to be a dietitian.'

Simon, ushering the dogs, leads the way inside.

Claire puts the kettle on. Dinah, eyes gleaming, takes a piece of flapjack from the plate ready on the table. 'It's good to be home, a pity I can't stay long.' 'Where is it you're going next?'

'Mainland Greece, not far from Athens.'

'We've been talking about going on a dig ourselves. We don't want to intrude on you, but we could find another one somewhere and then we could share our stories.'

'Talking about stories, in the common room, they were asking me about the Fairweathers. They thought I might have the lowdown on what happened to Sir Charles.'

'What did you say?' Simon frowns.

'Only that Lady F has gone to Scotland to grieve.'

‘Why do some people want to know the ins and outs of every occurrence?’ Claire rolls her eyes.

‘I thought I might call on Angus, see how he is.’

Simon raises an eyebrow. ‘Huh. I don’t think you need to worry about him. He’s gone on a cruise.’

13

June 1971

Angus parts from Toby at Southampton Central Station. Now that he is on his way home, he's anxious to arrive as soon as possible.

The journey to Whistledon is smooth; the train is running on time, and by 4.30pm he's striding down to the paddock. Nancy trots towards him and nuzzles his hand. It was a great cruise, but he's glad to be home. Giving Nancy a final pat, he makes his way to the stable block.

His smile fades as he enters Hebrew's stall. The horse whinnies as Angus strides towards him. He puts his hand on the horse's matted mane, strokes his dull coat. 'He's neglected you.' Anger rises in his chest. Looking around the stalls, Angus' shoulders droop; everywhere needs attention.

He sits on a chair in the corner, his head in his hands. Oh, Pa, where are you? He had forgotten how antiquated the stable block is, and it needs cleaning; Bill Bates hasn't kept on top of the job. Modernisation is going to take a lot of effort. He stands up and leans against Hebrew's flank, the horse shifts position gently. Still, once the work starts and Rodney is here, they will be able to make progress. He must get in touch with him very soon. It would be good if Toby joined them too, but that was up to him. He didn't want to push him. There'd be little pay for him until they had a good reputation for training.

The following morning, opening his eyes, Angus sits up immediately. Time to get up and start on the stable project. The plans crackle as he takes them out of the bureau in the library, unfolds them, looks at the costings. He had been relieved to find that the walls and roof are sound, there's no need to demolish anything. There is building to do to extend and refurbish. It will be good to get rid of the dark brown Victorian tiles with their curlicues. The walls will be lighter and brighter; it will be easier to make sure they're clean. Four more stalls seem ambitious enough for now. The builders will be here in two weeks. It's going to be disruptive and expensive. Meanwhile, he must prioritise Hebrew's well-being and training.

He pulls on his jacket and walks across to exercise the horse. He pats Hebrew standing patiently in the stall, lifts the saddle from the wall and heaves it onto the horse's back. 'Time for an outing.'

Cantering around the training field feels good; he's ready to start work. He isn't ready for the sudden rain or the loud claps of thunder. Hebrew pricks up his ears, flares his nostrils. Angus turns back towards the stables, reflecting what a steady horse Hebrew is. He isn't unduly disturbed. A good racehorse, not easily fazed by anything. It's going to stand him in good stead when the crowd are roaring him on.

They are both soaked. Angus discards his jacket then removes Hebrew's sodden tack and hangs it up. Turning to the horse, he begins to dry his coat and massage his muscles. It is important to keep him in good shape. The exercise helps to warm his own damp body.

Satisfied with his work, he strides towards the Hall to change his clothes.

On the terrace, Bill Bates is sweeping water away from a blocked drain. Roses are straggled across the path, brought down from the pergola by the force of the rain. They need to be tidied up again before someone trips. Bill is fully occupied; he needs to get that drain free. Some twine is all Angus needs. It will only take a moment.

As he goes towards the shed, he notes how dilapidated it is, ready for some creosote. He looks around the gardens, sees weeds choking flower beds, shrubs which have not been pruned.

As he turns the knob and opens the door, it catches on the ground, the hinges have dropped. He lifts the door, opening it wide, then takes a step backwards, something large is filling most of the floor space. His brow furrows: he moves forward. It's a wooden crate with foreign labelling, addressed to Pa. It had been opened but not unpacked. How long has it been there? The crate is sturdy, and it's some time before he's able to fully reveal the object inside; a garden ornament about three feet tall, a statue of Pan. Not quite the type of object he would've chosen for himself.

'Hey, Bill! What do you know about this?' Angus calls.

Bill comes across, scratching the back of his neck, his eyes opening wide as he realises that he has seen the crate before. 'I can't move that. Far too heavy.'

'I realise that.' Bill is beginning to show his age. The lines on his weather-beaten face are deeper, his hair a mess. 'Do you know where it came from?'

Bill shakes his head. 'It came on a lorry.'

Angus notices the hole in the sleeve of Bill's grubby sweater. Oh, shit, his wife died last year. A twinge of irritation runs through him. He needs younger workers. Ones who are on top of the job: there's a lot to do. 'Ok, thanks, Bill.' Angus finds the twine, ties up the roses and heads to the Hall.

Gertrude is waiting for him, her lips pursed. He raises his eyebrows.

'What's the problem, Gertrude?'

'This is.' She points to a large plaster on her hand. 'I was in the herb garden getting tarragon. Someone's been there with a knife and left it lying about.' She nods her head knowingly. 'I didn't see it until I'd cut myself.'

'What are you saying, Gertrude? Are you suggesting it was Bill?'

'Well, it wasn't Clive. We always use scissors.'

'Of course.'

‘I know Bill’s had a tough year but…’ she shrugs.
‘I understand.’

Whistledon Hall

July 1971

Dear Mother,

I have settled down to life at Whistledon now and have great ideas for the stables. Rodney, a groom, will be joining me from Brotherton. I have every confidence in his expertise and judgement.

The only fly in the ointment is Bill Bates. As you know, he was always very conscientious and reliable. However, he promised to look after the stables whilst I was away and, when I came back, Hebrew was unkempt and nervous. Thankfully, he's calmed down again now.

Unfortunately, Bill had received a crate marked FRAGILE whilst I was on the cruise. He'd opened it but not unpacked it to check the contents. He had just put it into the old shed and forgotten about it. I found it quite by chance.

Luckily, when I opened it, it seemed to be undamaged. It's a garden statue that, I hope when you are next here, you'll be able to suggest a place for. I don't know whether it was you or Father who ordered it in Istanbul. In the meantime, I've replaced it in the crate and left it in the shed.

I'm sorry but I've had to give Bill a verbal warning.

Otherwise, the estate seems to be running smoothly enough. And I need to get on with the developments. I think you will be quite excited by the scale of our plans.

Love,

Angus

Auchdair Castle

Dear Angus

I am pleased that you are feeling refreshed after the cruise. However, I am amazed that you gave Bill the job of looking after Hebrew whilst you were away. He is unused to handling horses and whereas you may gain comfort from their presence, I imagine he may have been overwhelmed by the responsibility, especially as his wife died recently. Please remember how very kind he was to you when you stayed at Whistledon in the school holidays - how much you used to enjoy helping him in the gardens.

I do hope that you will become a more understanding employer and treat him with kindness.

I am wondering if you are finding the horses more expensive than you expected and whether you ought to reconsider your plans to own and train racehorses.

The weather here is glorious at the moment, but the castle can seem dark and cold at times. It must be in contrast to the places that I have lived with your father. I was extremely fortunate until the awful happenings in Istanbul.

Do think carefully about your plans, perhaps it would be a good idea to ask the advice of Dominic. As a bishop, he is always anxious to fulfil his godparental duties and he does seem to have good sense.

My love as always,

Mother

14

July 1971

Simon closes the study door firmly and strides through into the kitchen. 'Phew, it's warm in here.'

Claire looks up from shaping dough into large scones.

'I'm going to walk down into the village and have a pint with Bill Bates. He's struggling with coming to terms with being made to retire; his pals are rallying round. He was saying that one of them would like a chat with me. It seems that I have my uses even if they don't come to church.'

Claire straightens her back and gives him a light kiss on the cheek. 'There, you *are* making a difference!'

'I'm not so sure about that. I saw the faces of the old guard after last week's sermon. They think I'm a heretic, when all I'm doing is trying to explain how I see Christianity now. Congregations are falling everywhere; we can't put our heads in the sand. I need to explain how it can fit in with today's science. Anyway, a drink might oil the cogs in my brain, I'm having difficulty in preparing anything for next Sunday.'

Claire smiles and pats his cheek with her floury hand. 'Make sure you don't stay too long.'

Wiping the flour off, he gives her a wry grin, 'It's ok, it's only a courtesy call.'

'Good to meet you rector. I hear you have some new ideas.'

Simon shakes the outstretched hand of the young man sitting next to Bill.

'I wonder who told you that? I don't think I've seen you in the congregation and Bill certainly isn't a churchgoer – yet.'

'My wife. She's one of the flower arrangers. She says you're more interesting than a lot of preachers.'

'What can I get you, Simon?' Bill stands, putting his hand in his pocket.

'Just a half of bitter, please.' Two other men are eyeing him up and down. He thinks they look like father and son. Both have the same curly hair. The young man's is dark and fashionably long, a proper mop-head; the older man's is grey and short above a lined face with pale blue watery eyes.

Bill puts a glass in front of him. 'We've been talking about death. My friend here, lost his wife, four years ago.' He glances up at the older man. 'I've been telling him that at her funeral, you said my wife had gone to a better place. How does anyone know?'

Simon puffs out his cheeks. 'Well, we don't of course, but sometimes in a near death experience....'

‘You mean when people nearly die and come back saying they’ve seen their body lying there?’

‘That’s right. They might see angels, or a tunnel filled with light.’

The three men nod.

‘The main thing they say is that they feel loved.’ Simon picks up his glass and tastes the ale. Good.

‘I’ve got an aunt who is a spiritualist medium. She passes messages.’ Why is he telling these men? He hasn’t been in touch with her for a while.

‘What about hell then?’

Simon blinks. ‘We create our own hell.’

Bill swallows a mouthful of beer.

An hour later, Simon is leaning over the bridge, staring into the waters of the Wye. Fixing his gaze on the odd leaf and stick, he watches as they float slowly on their way downstream. All is as it is. He doesn’t need to push against the establishment. Gradually, bit by bit he will make progress, he will get there. He can give matters a gentle nudge, speak his truth. He isn’t the only one, others will join him. He hopes. Pushing against the rough stone, he straightens up and turns to walk back up the road to the rectory.

15

Auchdair

12th August 1971

The castle is home to paying guests. Elspeth wishes it were otherwise. “Necessary for the upkeep of the place,” says hardnosed Robbie. They are gathered in the gunroom.

‘The Glorious Twelfth is the biggest shoot of the year. My sister shoots well. Elspeth was one of the best when she was young.’ He opens a gun cupboard, placing the rifle on the table.

She picks it up, feeling its weight, much heavier than a revolver. Can she keep her hands steady enough to aim straight? ‘I’m very out of practice. I might not join you.’

Robbie frowns. ‘I do hope you will.’

He is insisting she joins in this year, saying she can’t hide herself away, the locals want to see her. Elspeth doesn't think they do, unless they want to see how much she's changed since Charles was killed. People can be cruel.

Robbie unlocks two more guns for his guests, and the little party assembles outside ready to walk up to the butts.

Elspeth closes her eyes, stands still, the sound of the feet crunching on the gravelly ground gradually recedes. She can't do it. She turns around and walks back. Standing in her path is Robbie.

'Have you forgotten something, Elspeth?'

'Oh yes, I won't be a minute. I'll catch you up.'

'I'll wait for you.'

Her legs weaken. She can't let Robbie know why she can't fire a gun. Clinging to the banister, she climbs the stairs to her room, takes a handkerchief out of her pocket, blows her nose, returns.

He smiles, 'We can walk up together now.'

The morning is bright, the heather a vibrant purple in the sun. Elspeth looks around, focusing on her surroundings, the mountains high around the valley, a stream trickling along its rocky bed. Gratitude for what she has. She's barely aware of Robbie chatting.

She turns to him, 'I don't think I can shoot anymore.' Those poor birds will feel the shot and fall hard on the ground and be picked up by a dog. 'It all seems barbaric to me now.'

Robbie stops. 'You're being irrational. The birds are killed almost instantly. The dogs have very soft mouths, they don't damage the kill. We need food to eat, we are omnivores. Be pragmatic. See the world as it is.'

'I can't do it.'

‘Come on Elspeth, we can't let our paying guests down. Brace yourself, you are a Farquhar after all.’

She takes three deep breaths, Charles would say, “It’s duty, Elspeth. Stiff upper lip and all that.” Her heart is sinking, but she must put on a good show. The butts are in sight.

Arriving, Elspeth looks around. One of the women calls to Robbie, needing advice. Elspeth pictures how she used to be, firing accurately, killing the birds, making sure they didn't fly away wounded. She doesn't feel able to shoot, but she opens the gun and loads the cartridges, looks around again. Robbie finishes instructing and looks across at her, his brow wrinkling. She smiles. He turns back to the young woman as she fires at the grouse, almost overhead, and misses completely. The sound makes Elspeth stand rigid; her teeth clenched. She unloads the gun and puts it down.

Robbie sees what she's doing, mutters to himself, cursing his stupidity. Charles was shot for goodness’ sake. Why on earth would he put his dear sister through this?

In Whistledon, Angus strokes Hebrew’s nose, turns impatiently and walks to the car. He hasn't time to go to Auchdair, but Uncle Robbie has said that Ma is very much on edge. He’s insisting he visit.

Driving through the parkland, he notices a sheep hobbling. He must mention it to the farm manager. How often does he check the flock? At least he has no qualms about leaving Hebrew in Rodney's care. He must remember to fill in the papers for the race. Glancing at the speedometer, he takes his foot off the accelerator.

The miles pass, he concentrates; in his flying days, he learned to relax and concentrate. He remembers the thrill of piloting. Maybe when the stables are successful, he'll buy a plane, use it to get to race meetings. He wishes he had one now, it's a long journey.

The sun is setting by the time he arrives in Auchdair. Driving up the winding estate road, he sees the silhouette of the castle, dark against the evening sky. It isn't a large building but as always, he's impressed by its forbidding presence. His mind flicks back to the Hall with its long low building; how lucky he is to live there. He sits for a moment, readying himself to talk to Ma. He sighs, grimaces, takes a deep breath and lowers his feet onto the crunchy gravel.

Angus is pleased to see her bright face, but she looks smaller than she did. He bends down to kiss her cheek, sniffs a trace of whisky, but hey, he's looking forward to a dram himself.

He smiles, feels in his pocket, brings out an envelope, 'I've brought some photos of the new stable block – and more importantly, the horses.' He passes it to her. 'I know you've been worrying about what we're doing.'

'I don't know who told you that, I trust your judgement. Although I did think it a little extravagant when you went on a cruise.'

Angus frowns. 'Perhaps it was, but I feel better for getting away.'

She nods, turns her attention to the photographs. 'They look good, though I'm no expert.'

Angus grins. 'Dominic taught me well.'

'Have you seen much of him?'

'I have. He says he's doing his Godfatherly duties. In fact, the grey is named after him.'

'The Godfather?'

Angus shakes his head.

'The bishop?'

'Gregorian Chants.'

Elspeth smiles. 'I like that. And the other horse?'

'Another three-year-old colt. Jericho.'

She raises her eyebrows. Biblical? Did Dominic help with the names? 'I look forward to watching them race.'

Over dinner, Angus thinks his mother seems as normal as can be expected in the circumstances; just a little withdrawn, less talkative than she used to be. After a few glasses of wine, he decides to mention his plans to employ someone younger.

'I've had to let Bill go.'

Elspeth sits back, 'Angus! That's too bad of you.'

He leans his elbows on the table and looks directly into her eyes. 'He's a liability; Gertrude cut herself on a knife he'd left amongst the herbs'

'After all those years of service, all those holidays when he let you help him in the garden.'

'The shed is falling down, and there's a crate in there, that he'd forgotten about.'

'The poor man.'

This wasn't the moment to mention Clive saying Bill was worse for wear in the Blacksmiths Arms most nights. 'There's a statue in the crate.'

Elspeth frowns.

'It's addressed to Pa.'

'Put it out of sight.' she hisses. 'Hide it. I don't want to hear any more about it.' She stands up and leaves the room.

16

Whistledon on Wye

September 1971

Claire puts the phone down, her heart pounding. 'Did she say the right things? What did she say?' Dinah sounded very much in control, wants to come home and bring her baby with her. Matthew, her baby!

She sits on the chair by the telephone table as the facts sink in. She has a grandson. No wonder Dinah hasn't been home for five months. She asks herself why she didn't notice last time Dinah came for the weekend. Thinks back, nods, pictures the new jazzy loose top she was wearing. Why hadn't Dinah told her? Is she such a judgemental mother? It's exciting, but what about Dinah's degree studies? She was very evasive about the father.

She realises Dinah has chosen to phone when Simon is at Evening Prayers. 'What's the best way to tell him? It will be difficult for some of the parishioners to accept that their rector has a daughter who has had a child out of wedlock. She can imagine the look on the face of the chairman of the Mother's Union, frosty at the best of times.

She wanders back into the kitchen, mechanically picks up the knife she had been using, and continues to chop the onion. Blinks her eyes as the onion affects them; allows tears to course down her cheeks, glad of the excuse to cry.

Stirring a pan of risotto on the stove, she hears Simon whistling softly as he comes in, turns towards him. He kisses her on the cheek, 'I have some news for you.'

'Oh. Bad news?'

'Not really... but it might be a problem for you and the parishioners.'

Simon frowns. 'I think you'd better just tell me.'

'Ok.' She removes the pan and looks him in the eyes. 'Dinah phoned. She has a baby. A boy. Matthew.'

Simon's jaw clenches, he holds his breath, then with eyes widening says, 'What the hell! Who is the father? A fellow Pagan?'

'She wouldn't name him.'

He sighs.

'She's coming home tomorrow so we'll find out more then.'

He nods. 'Good. Not before time. Surely, she didn't give birth on the archaeological dig?'

'She didn't go on it.'

'What? She lied to us?'

'She didn't want to worry us. She's in a home for unmarried mothers.'

'A home for unmarried mothers. They can be dreadful places.' Simon clasps his head. 'Do you remember that poor girl at St Mary's? Her child was put up for adoption. She was devastated.' He paces the kitchen. 'I can't believe she's been so irresponsible.'

'I don't suppose she intended to become pregnant.' Claire smiles. 'I'm looking forward to meeting the little fellow.'

'A grandson. Well, we must look after him, whoever his father is.'

He opens the cupboard. 'I think we should have a sherry before we eat.'

Simon hears the car draw up outside, stands, puts his hands in his pockets, clenches his fists and looks out of the window.

Dinah inside the taxi, puts Matthew back into his carrycot whispering, 'It's going to be all right.'

Matthew's eyes open wide, and he gives a little whimper.

Claire is running down the path to the taxi, holding open the door whilst Dinah lifts out the cot. Claire turns to the baby. 'What a beautiful boy you are!'

Dinah gives a sigh of relief. He's going to be loved; she is still loved.

Simon follows, puts an arm around Dinah and takes the carrycot. My little girl is a mother, a woman now, the baby must be welcomed. It is not his fault that he is a bastard. He pushes the word down. He is a surprise, a welcome surprise. He bends and touches the soft skin of the tiny cheeks, puts his finger into the very small hand. The baby curls his fingers around it. God is good.

Dinah looks him in the eye, obviously wondering what he is thinking.

He feels a surge of love and appreciation. Claire, tears running down her cheeks, is holding Dinah as if she can't believe that she is home. The baby gives a little cry. Dinah bends down and picks him up.

'Meet Matthew, my unplanned little miracle. I'm hoping that you will love him as much as I do.'

'It's good you've come home. Little boys need a man about the house.'

Dinah draws herself up, bristling, 'That's not always possible. A strong woman will do.'

Simon blinks. 'Yes, I'm sure you will do as good a job as you can. It's not easy bringing up a child.'

Dinah turns back to Claire. 'Let's go inside, I'm ready for a cup of tea and then you can hold him.'

Simon scratches his head; he doesn't want to fall out with Dinah, but she needs to realise how hard it will be if the child doesn't have a father. A thought sweeps through him. Was she raped? That is a whole different take on the situation. He can't ask her. Or can he? He follows them into the house, puts the kettle on, looks at Dinah, trying to read her expression. Is she happy? She obviously loves her little boy. Perhaps she loves his father?

'I'm perplexed as to why you're reluctant to name the father.'

'He doesn't know. I need to tell him before anyone else.'

Simon rolls his eyes. 'The poor chap's in for a big surprise. I don't understand, you've had months...'

Claire glares at him.

'Perhaps you think it is better to tell him face to face.' He imagines the gossip spreading. 'Whereabouts does he live? We can take you in the car if it's a long journey.'

Dinah smiles.

Simon watches Claire holding the little boy, her hand cradling the small head. with its light brown wisps of hair, the fontanel pulsing gently. They had wanted a boy as well as a girl, but it wasn't to be. Now she's obviously very happy. 'No. You must make yourself at home here. Young Matthew is a blessing.'

Dinah's shoulders relax; tears spring to her eyes.

Claire turns and kisses Simon's cheek, 'Here, you hold him while I mash the tea.'

He gently supports the baby's neck as he clasps him close, breathing in the familiar 'baby-smell' from Christenings. Not something he's going to mention to Dinah.

The Rectory

Whistledon

September 1971

Dear Aunt Violet,

I hope that you are well and keeping busy in retirement.

We have some exciting news. Dinah has come home for a while, she has a son, a beautiful baby boy. She has called him Matthew, after Father. I hope he would be pleased if he was still with us.

Dinah is intent on raising him on her own, without the help of his father.

We look forward to your visit at Christmas.

With love,

Simon and Claire

Leeds

September 1971

Dear Simon and Claire,

How wonderful that you have a grandson, and for him to be named after his great grandfather. It will be lovely to see you all at Christmas.

As you know, my brother Matthew never thought much of my beliefs. I doubt he's changed, but who knows? Perhaps he thinks differently now.

We have Sunday Services and spiritual healing sessions twice a week, so I am keeping busy and well.

Much love,

Aunt Violet

17

Whistledon on Wye

October 1971

A storm is brewing. Angus, riding Nancy, avoids the woods, where the tree branches are waving wildly in the wind. He has left the horses in the paddock; he wants to get them back into their stalls before they become agitated. It isn't Hebrew that he is concerned about, but the two younger ones can be skittish.

He's been across to the most distant farm because the tenant wanted to see him personally. Angus doesn't want to be pestered with petty details, but this chap obviously needs help. He's not sure what he can do about mental health problems. He rode Nancy hoping that the journey would relax him, but that hasn't worked; he knows he is becoming increasingly angry about being left to deal with all the estate problems, as well as trying to develop the stables. Has he bitten off more than he can chew? Pa shouldn't have gone to Istanbul, when he said he was going to settle down and get the work done on the stables. Nobody has been arrested for the assassination, nor has a name even been suggested. He prods Nancy to get a move on as they skirt the trees. The pony responds briefly but then begins to limp

Angus pulls her to a halt and dismounts to examine her hooves. He can see what the trouble is, an old bramble has become entangled. He extricates it as well as he can, but knows it needs a good light and some tweezers. He begins to lead her home steadily; there's a good mile to go. The wind is gusting even more; the clouds are blowing across and it won't be long before the sun sets. He clenches his jaw, trudges along, Nancy carrying one leg gingerly.

At last, they enter the estate. Gregorian Chants and Jericho are cantering wildly about the paddock; he sighs and hurries Nancy along. Opening the gate of the paddock Angus, leading Nancy back in, catches sight of Dinah coming towards him across the grass.

'Angus, I really need to talk to you.'

'Can't it wait? I need to call the vet.'

'No. We have a son. Matthew.'

It takes Angus a few moments to digest what she's said. He stands legs apart, hands on hips. 'It's not mine.'

'You do remember we had sex on Christmas Eve?'

'Of course I bloody do.'

'I've been away, or I would have told you earlier.'

'Doesn't make any difference. It's bollocks. The bastard isn't mine.'

For a moment, Dinah shrinks back. 'Typical. You want the fun but not the responsibility.'

'Look, this is fucking ridiculous. I need to call the vet.' Turning his back on her he strides towards the Hall. Dinah swivels on her heels and hikes off in the other direction, muttering.

Simon carefully puts his communion vessels back into their case. The old farmworker shakes his hand, thanks him, hobbles to the door and opens it for him. He's been retired for some time now; years of hard physical labour have taken their toll.

Simon walks back to the rectory reflecting that the Fairweathers, like most gentlemen farmers, have never soiled their own hands. He wonders if that's changing now that the present one is actively involved in training racehorses.

He remembers Claire will be out; she had asked Dinah if she could take Matthew into the Church Hall to meet the ladies of the Mother's Union. She was wanting to show them that their little boy has been accepted into the family with love. To his surprise, Dinah agreed very quickly, thanking Claire and saying that she had something she needed to do.

As he approaches the house, he can hear the dogs barking wildly. Reaching the kitchen, he finds two frenetic animals, their paws upon the windowsill, looking out. Following the direction of their gaze, he sees two horses galloping away, back up the hill.

Smashed and splintered planks are lying on the grass and the patio. Anger rises in his chest. The boundary fence is wrecked. He rushes out of the door; the dogs push past him and charge up the hill after the horses. He stands, seething, amidst the debris, the soil churned up by flailing hooves, Claire's precious herbs uprooted and strewn around.

18

God! What a day! Angus picks up a shovel and begins to clear out Hebrew's stall. If only he could shovel all the shit out of his life!

He's hardly slept. Bloody Dinah causing so much trouble in such a short space of time. Thank God the horses aren't hurt. She could have totally ruined the plans. He picks up another shovelful and throws it into the barrow. He'll feel better for doing this. What has she told her parents? It can't be his; he hopes. What a bloody cheek! That fence is a mess; she left the gate open. Goodness knows what he called her. Does he need to apologise to that smug rector? He refuses to go to the rectory. He'll send a letter.

Throwing the last load onto the steaming pile, he wipes his shirt sleeve across his brow, props the shovel against the wall and heads to the Hall for breakfast

Upper Whistledon Hall

September 1971

Dear Rector,

I regret the need to write. However, I had a disturbing encounter with your daughter yesterday, which made me extremely angry. I apologise for the uncharacteristic language that I used, but I was under extreme provocation. Dinah was quite out of order with her allegations. I must protest. I don't wish to break her confidence, but I was, and remain, extremely shocked.

It was unfortunate that my valuable horses entered your garden. I'm relieved to say they remain unharmed. The fence will be repaired in due time.

Yours faithfully,

Angus Fairweather

In his study, Simon splits open the envelope and reads. Face flushing, he leaps up and dashes into the kitchen looking for Claire. Not finding her, he takes a deep breath, re-reads the letter and returns to his desk.

The Rectory

Dear Sir Angus,

Your behaviour is unpardonable. Your horses appear to try and jump any fence they see. Our herb garden is totally ruined.

You will receive the bill for the damage done to the car and the herb garden. as soon as we have the assessor's report.

Regards,

Simon Shorthouse

Claire is sitting on the patio, soaking up the sun's rays. Deliberately closing her eyes to the churned-up soil of the herb bed. The sound of a tractor and the accompanying smell mean one of the Fairweathers' men is spraying slurry in the lower pasture. Through the gap in the broken fence, she can see the tractor pulling a dilapidated looking slurry tank. The joys of living in the country! The autumn sun is giving a pleasant heat with no need to seek the shade. The day is passing, and she, Claire, has nothing to show for it; she must stir herself.

She stands, shaking the tension from her arms. She'll make chutney; that will be a useful distraction from her worries about Dinah. Tomato chutney is one of Simon's favourites. Stopping midway down the path, she admires the rosehips, pale orange to bright red, noticing that two white flowers are still on the bush. Everything and everyone at their own stage in life. This one will pass. Chutney will bring a smile to Simon's face. He needs cheering up after the debacle with the horses.

She makes her way into the greenhouse, fortunately unscarred. What might have happened to the racehorses if they had broken the panes? The tomato plants are still producing a few red fruit but a lot are unripe and needing to be used. She picks a basketful and makes her way towards the house.

As she reaches the back door, Simon comes out waving an envelope.

'He's not getting away with his high-handed behaviour. Does he call that an apology! An apology is not enough! Back in a minute.'

Claire looks up as Simon comes in. 'What was all that about?'

'Angus Fairweather blaming Dinah for his horses wrecking the fence.'

She frowns. 'Did she frighten them? Racehorses can be very nervous.'

'Apparently, she made some allegations. That's hardly an excuse for his horses damaging the car and destroying your herb garden.'

She glances up. 'I can replant that. What allegations? You don't think Angus Fairweather is...?'

'Matthew's father?' He puffs out his cheeks. 'Who knows?'

Upper Whistledon Hall

Dear Rector,

I can only express disappointment at your reply to my apology. You call my behaviour unpardonable. I wonder how you square that with your conscience and Christian ideals. Particularly as I've promised recompense in the fullness of time. I acknowledge that my reaction to Dinah's plea for me to be recognised as the father of her child was not as gentle and sympathetic as, in hindsight, I'd wish. Quite the opposite in fact. I was forcible in expressing my feelings as to her promiscuity.

I realise that I'm not totally innocent but hope that you're able to forgive me when you recognise the pressure that I was placed under.

I'm sure that when Bishop Gregory dines with me soon, he will give me his usual wise advice.

Kind regards,

Angus

Simon runs his hands through his hair. 'Claire!'

She comes scuttling from the kitchen. 'Whatever is the matter?'

'Look. Angus Fairweather is going too far.' He hands her the letter, breathing heavily. 'He seems to be admitting some guilt.'

She touches his arm. 'Let me have a word with her before you reply.'

Simon glares. 'He should have known better. He's going to have a strong letter, regardless of the bishop.'

The Rectory

Dear Sir Angus,

Dinah assures me that she has not had intimate relations with any of the students at university. Your actions on Christmas Eve were reprehensible; plying her with alcohol when my wife and I left your soirée early to prepare for the Midnight Service was the mark of a lout. As was giving the rest of the staff the evening off, clearing the way for you to assault her in the kitchen on the pretext of fetching ice for drinks.

Although I wish it otherwise, I am reconciled to the fact that you are my grandson's father.

Your selfish, thoughtless behaviour has had life-changing consequences for my daughter. She has had to withdraw from Oxford.

I agree that it would be useful to inform the bishop of your new status. I am praying that you will soon acknowledge your responsibilities.

Regards,

Simon Shorthouse

Bollocks! It's hardly his fault the girl threw herself on him. It's time she was allowed to do what she feels like doing, not be bound by rules from some religion she doesn't believe in and it's nothing to do with Reverend Simon.

Upper Whistledon Hall

Dear Rector,

I understand your wish to protect your daughter, and I don't want to be unkind to her, but Dinah can't have been frank with you. I suspect she was attempting to manipulate me. It would undoubtedly be to her advantage if she were to marry into a respected family with some wealth.

However, I recommend that you question her again. I am confident that the father is someone else.

Regards,

Angus Fairweather

The Rectory

Dear Sir Angus,

It is regretful that you seem able to easily dismiss the life of a child that might be yours, leaving my daughter with the responsibility for his care.

You obviously have no loving feelings towards Dinah. I think it would be advisable not to approach her again.

Your suggestion that Dinah may have sought pregnancy to marry into your family is a figment of your pride and imagination.

Being as you are considerably older than Dinah, and have much more experience of the world, I would have hoped you would have behaved with consideration and respect. Instead, you treated her disgracefully and now continue to compound your actions with heartless words. I find your attitude irresponsible and immoral.

I am confident that the bishop will have some good advice for you.

Regards,

Simon Shorthouse

Angus, resisting the urge to screw up the letter, drops it on the table.

Upper Whistledon Hall

Dear Rector,

I'm relieved to know that Dinah has no designs upon an inheritance for her child. I'm willing to take a paternity test, which I'm sure will prove negative. I was told that I'm infertile, the result of mumps I suffered about three years ago. This means, of course, that the estate will pass to my sister's child. The irony being that I caught the infection from him. It was a blow at first, but looking at things positively, it means that I'm free to remain a bachelor. If by any miracle Dinah's child is mine, I'll honour my obligations and provide for him, including a suitable education. Matthew would inherit in due course.

In the meantime, Dinah needs to be open with you about any other men who could be the father of her child.

I think that you'll find the stigma attached to single mothers has disappeared and the State will be helpful. I'm sure that if Dinah has parental support young Matthew will thrive.

Regards,

Angus Fairweather

Simon shakes his head, ‘How dare he presume to know anything about the stigma around unmarried mothers? He lives in a totally different world. They have the money to keep things quiet.’ He passes the letter to Claire. ‘It’s beginning to look as if he can’t be Matthew’s father, but Dinah needs to know for sure. She must accept the offer of a paternity test.’

‘I’m just glad we’re able to help and that Dinah is happy being a mother. Matthew is lovely, and he’s contented, generally.’

Simon stands up, ‘If it is his child, Dinah must make sure that Matthew is brought up properly in a loving home, not sent off to boarding school to toughen him up. The upper class have some funny ideas.’

‘I’m sure Dinah will insist that he has the education she wants. Though, I suppose we don’t know anything about the other man and his background.’ Claire sighs. ‘I hope she tells us. I’m still upset that Dinah chose to go into a home rather than come here.’

‘I suspect she was wanting to avoid the scandal. Impossible to do that now.’

The Rectory

Dear Sir Angus,

It is unfortunate you have been rendered infertile, if that is the case, but I am saddened that you seem to see this as a source of sexual liberty. Relationships are what matter in life, not lustful brief encounters.

We are pleased to accept the offer of a paternity test to confirm the position.

I am attaching the assessor's report on our car and look forward to the full settlement at your earliest convenience.

Regards,

Simon

Upper Whistledon Hall

Dear Simon,

I shall arrange my part of the paternity test immediately. I shall be pleased to be able to refute Dinah's claim.

It is regretful that your daughter has become promiscuous, her protected childhood must have caused her naivety.

I'll be dining with Bishop Gregory tomorrow. After we've discussed the horses, I'll ask him to pray for her.

Kind regards, Angus

'There he goes again. He knows nothing about the way we've brought up Dinah.' Striding into the lounge, Simon hands the letter to Claire. Raising her eyebrows, she puts down her knitting to read. She gasps.

'Is that what people are saying?'

'It's all very well for you to coo over young Matthew, and for Dinah to name him after my father, but I need to maintain a show of dignity and morality.'

He paces to the window. 'If the bishop thinks I'm not behaving in a Christian way, my place here might become untenable.' He turns and looks at Claire, 'Money talks and the parish can't afford to lose its chief benefactor.'

She frowns. 'Do you think Dinah was lonely?'

'I think her Pagan friends led her astray.'

With a heavy sigh, Simon closes the rectory door firmly. He needs time to think. The night was disturbed by the baby's crying. Claire wanted to help, but he persuaded her to let Dinah take the responsibility.

She needs to realise that bringing up a child takes patience and effort. His own patience is still being tested. When they arrived at St Peters it seemed an ideal situation. He'd been proud that Dinah had a place at Oxford, expecting that she would relish the experience, as he had done at Cambridge. But within weeks of being there she'd become a Pagan. He'd coped with the reactions to that. Now, not only has she compromised his position further, but she's thrown away her avenue to a good career by becoming an unmarried mother. To make things worse, she's had sex with Angus Fairweather, who obviously has no respect for her. He realises this irks him more than it should. She's undermining his position. His reputation.

As he reaches the church, the dogs bound towards the verger who's sweeping fallen hazelnuts off the path. The unripe nuts bounce waywardly, with the force of the brush, before coming to rest in the long grass between the gravestones. Simon calls the dogs to heel; they come at once.

Upper Whistledon Hall

Dear Simon,

I am pleased to enclose a copy of the paternity test as promised. The results are as I expected.

My best wishes to Dinah and Matthew.

Yours sincerely,

Angus

Simon leans against the Aga holding the letter in his hand. ‘Looks like Angus was right; Matthew isn't his son. Not quite as embarrassing as it might have been. We need to tell her.’

Claire drops the tea towel onto the table, calls upstairs to Dinah who is in her bedroom, feeding Matthew. ‘We need you to come down.’

‘I’ll be there soon.’

‘Let’s hope this other fellow cares about her. Young men shouldn't go around sowing their seed and not taking responsibility for the consequences.’ He looks out into the garden, then bends down to pat Spike. ‘You can't do that old boy can you. Irresponsible, that's what it is.’

‘I don’t think she wants to marry the other man.’

He frowns. ‘What gives you that idea?’

‘For a start, she won't tell us who he is.’

Simon clenches his teeth. ‘We can't afford to bring him up forever.’

‘She'll probably see sense and tell us more when she's ready.’

‘I hope you’re right.’

Claire steps forward to take Matthew as Dinah comes in.

'What is it now?'

'You need to read this.'

'Oh, perhaps that's a good thing. He wasn't very nice to me.'

'Will you tell the other man now?'

Dinah shakes her head. I can't and I won't.

'Dinah, you need to be practical. Children are expensive. Rectors' salaries aren't generous.'

'I know. I'll have to get a job. I've got friends, they will help, if you don't want me here.'

Claire sees the petulant expression on Dinah's face. 'There's no need to be huffy. We're doing our best. I'm fully employed without any wages.'

The Rectory,

Dear Angus,

Thank you for your letter with the test results.

You must be very relieved to know that your encounter with my daughter has proved unproductive. She is not cooperating as well as I would wish. She refuses to name anyone else.

My concern for my daughter has coloured my thinking. My position as rector is another difficulty. We in the clergy, try to uphold the morals in the community and of course I have always done my best to set a good example. Boys brought up without a father lack a role model. Claire will help Dinah as much as she will allow but she is talking of leaving to be near her friends.

I trust that our disagreements can be put behind us for the sake of the parish. It is good that you with your standing, and me in my position, can be seen as good role models.

Simon shows the letter to Claire.

She laughs. 'You can be very pompous. Why don't you just phone him and say thanks for your help?'

Simon scowls. I don't think that's appropriate. Besides, he may bc busy, or out.'

19

Whistledon on Wye

December 1971

Angus turns off the engine. His mother stirs. She's been asleep for the last fifty miles. Thank goodness she relaxed at last. She was distracting, talking about refusing Robbie's offer of a cottage because she's needed here as the lady of the house. Is she right? Will he never marry? He isn't sure.

Opening her eyes, she gives a quick shake of her head and smiles as she takes in the warm lights of the Hall. It's good to be back but without Charles it's a different place, empty. Her heart sinks at the thought of the services and Mothers' Union party she's expected to attend.

Gertrude, her round face wreathed in smiles, comes rushing out of the door. 'How wonderful that you are home again.'

She smiles tenuously 'I'm very lucky that Angus was able to spare the time to fetch me.'

'I'll bring tea to the little sitting room.'

The Hall is quiet. Climbing the stairs, Elspeth passes the familiar portraits. Angus has asked her if she wants to choose one of Charles to add. She'll think about it. In their bedroom, she straightens her shoulders, changes her jacket for a cardigan and hurries down to the little sitting room.

A fire is burning in the grate. The side table is laid with a plate of Welsh cakes and shortbread. Elspeth takes her flask out of her handbag ready to lace her tea. Angus hasn't followed her into the house. Immediately, he'd walked to the stables to check on the horses.

Later, sitting in the dining room, she imagines Charles in his usual place, turning towards her, handing her a glass of wine.

Angus is quiet, focusing on the steak pie on his plate, a beer in front of him. He gives her an encouraging smile but leaves her to pick up the bottle of red wine. She pours another glass, drinks deeply, the smooth liquid trickles down her throat, relaxing her. She wants to think straight, needs to plan carefully. She must hide it. She can't leave it in her case any longer. If Gertrude discovers it in the bedroom, goodness knows what will happen. Why did she do that terrible thing? It has haunted her ever since. If she hadn't acted so impulsively, she would not be tormented now.

At first light Elspeth pulls on her wellingtons, her heart beating fast, she breathes deeply trying to calm down. She stands, the gun weighing heavy in her waterproof jacket, hands trembling, she closes the front door softly, takes another deep breath. Somebody might be watching; she must not go straight there. She makes her way towards the stables, then across to the drystone boundary wall.

A few sheep are nibbling the wet grass; one raises her head and stares. Elspeth's eyes are wide, scanning the area around. She chooses a gnarled hawthorn tree as a marker and sidles behind it. The branches snag on her clothing. The wall is rough to her bare hands. She chooses a small stone, wrestles it out, places the gun into the gap, pushing it in as far as possible before repairing the hole. The weight gone, she hurries on, rounding the end of the wall, heading towards the Hall. She doesn't look back until she reaches the paddock.

Nancy sees her and comes to the fence. Elspeth pauses, stroking the horse's neck, allows her eyes to rest on the hawthorn tree. She stiffens. The tall pale figure disappears. She shakes her head. Did she imagine it?

20

There is a hushed buzz as Elspeth enters the softly lit church. The children from the village school are holding their Christingle oranges, their candles unlit. She has seen few people from the village or the estate since her return from Scotland. She hopes to be uplifted by the church where she said her final goodbyes to Charles. She needs to concentrate on the children. Her eyes scan across the small figures, coming to rest upon a short girl with long blonde plaits, fixes them on the red bow resting on a navy cardigan. She suddenly screws up her eyes, closing them at the vivid memory of Charles' red blood seeping through his shirt. She must go back to the hymn sheet, keep calm. Looking up, she is aware of the rector's eyes upon her. As his forehead wrinkles, their eyes meet. She forces a smile. He turns away, moving his attention to the main body of the church.

'Welcome everyone. I expect many of you are excited at the thought of Christmas. Today, we are going to celebrate the reason we have that feast: the arrival of baby Jesus. He came to bring light to the world.' Simon holds a Christingle aloft. 'We light candles to symbolise this. Shall we do that now?'

The oranges are clasped firmly as the candles are lit.

'Now we can sing "Give me oil in my lamp, keep me burning." We are being reminded that we can all be a light in our own corner of the world. We can all bring love and joy to the people around us.' Simon gestures encouragingly to the children waiting to sing. The voices ring out as the oranges are held up. Elspeth joins in enthusiastically with her strong contralto voice. Suddenly, as the words "give me peace in my heart" hit her consciousness, she sees a figure slump to the ground. The sensation is overwhelming. She can't read the hymn sheet clearly. Her voice falters. Tears are streaming down her cheeks. She can't sing, is panting for breath. Claire's hand is upon her arm, steadying her. The moment passes. She is back in the church, needing to control herself in front of the children. The rector is saying "please be seated." She sits. The rest of the service is a blur.

As she turns to go out, Claire is inviting her to stay for a cup of tea in the church hall. She needs to be alone, to sort herself out. Compose herself. A whisky will help. She shakes her head. 'Gertrude will have tea ready for me. Thank you.'

Climbing into her car, she clutches the wheel, sighs and begins the drive back to the Hall, her cheeks reddening; Claire saw her tears. Charles would expect her to be stronger.

Clive, heading to the pub for his evening shift, swears loudly when his old Vauxhall backfires again.

Gertrude has been reminding him that it's due for a service; she'll have heard that and will be nagging.

Elspeth is passing the Lodge, its emptiness echoing her own, when she hears the sound of a shot.

Charles is crumpling to the ground beside her. Fresh bright blood on his clean white shirt.

Her eyes close, the car lurching to the left, brushes the bushes at the side of the drive. She jerks the steering wheel hard, just missing the fence on the right. Putting her foot down firmly on the accelerator, she shoots up the hill, almost colliding with the car coming down.

Clive sees headlights coming towards him, a car swerving from side to side, narrowly misses him. He brakes, gasping for breath, gripping the wheel. 'What the fuck?' Has she been drinking? Better tell Angus to have a word before she kills someone.

Trembling uncontrollably, Elspeth arrives at the Hall. Breathing deeply, trying to calm herself, she sees Gertrude drawing the curtains in the little sitting room. Movement catches her attention as she looks towards the lawn. To her horror, someone is walking across it, a tall, pearlescent figure. Ice pours through her veins as the figure pauses, stares directly at her. She scrambles from the car and sprints into the house, slamming the door. She's safe... Or is she? Will she ever be safe again?

'Good evening.' Gertrude's eyes widen. 'Are you all right? I'll bring the tea, that'll warm you up.'

Elspeth forces a smile, drifts through to the sitting room, pours herself a whisky and sinks into her chair.

Clive is still frowning when he steps behind the bar. Seeing Bill Bates coming to be served, he grins and starts to pull his usual pint. He won't mention Elspeth's driving. Bill's fond of the mistress and has enough of his own problems.

Bill fishes in his pocket for cash. 'I hear young Angus has bought more racehorses. No wonder he can't afford to pay me. *She* wouldn't have sacked me.' He waits for the froth to settle, before taking a sip. 'Got more money than sense.'

'Maybe. I have to say they look good, but we'll have to see how they run.'

Bill turns away to sit in the snug with his domino-playing friends.

21

January 1972

It is too quiet now that Katrina and the children have gone home. It was good to have them here for Christmas.

Looking across at Angus' strained face, Elspeth wonders what he's thinking. He's not saying much but she knows he will do very soon.

How can she explain herself? She hadn't felt sleepy, the night was bright, she didn't want to go to bed until she was tired enough to go to sleep. Charles is in her mind She misses him. He should have been here playing with his grandchildren. She'd thought a walk would tire her out. She leans back in her chair, waiting.

Angus takes a few grapes to go with his cheese and biscuits, and asks, 'Are you going to tell me what you were doing last night?' There's a slight pause before he adds, 'You can't go wandering about in the dark, frightening the horses.' Looking at her, he pops two grapes into his mouth.

Sitting back, eyes open wide, she says nothing. She can't tell him about the shadowy figure and how it walked into the stable wall.

'No. No, I won't. I didn't do anything. I was only having a walk.'

'Ok.' Taking another grape, he pushes back his chair. 'I'll see you later.'

22

Simon twirls his pen carefully and deliberately. The monthly meeting with the Parochial Church Council was difficult again. Why did Elspeth tell the Mothers' Union yoga class that Epiphany celebrates Jesus' baptism? How well-informed is she? He sighs, begins to write, crosses it out, puts down his pen and stretches his arms. It's doubtful that the Sunday morning congregation will be in the mood for information out of the ordinary. Some of them come because they think it pleases God, others to see friends, and then there are of course, those that simply enjoy singing.

He looks out of the window at the heavy frost on the path. He wants to deliver new ideas, but he needs to choose where and when. Better stick to his usual sermon, saying Epiphany marks the arrival of the Wise Men at the birth of Jesus. Perhaps he can hold discussions in the evenings. He smiles; maybe Elspeth's interference will be helpful in the long run. The parish is thriving in many ways: The Mothers' Union and Young Wives are well attended, The Youth Club extremely active. St Peters does seem to be at the centre of social life in the village, together with the Blacksmiths Arms. Perhaps discussions will help to fulfil the spiritual needs of his parishioners, and even his own.

He picks up his prayer book, opening it at the General Confession. He can't agree that we are all miserable sinners as the book has it. We all have choices and sometimes we regret the ones we've made.

Jesus taught compassion for the outcast. He didn't ask them to grovel but to follow him, enjoy, rejoice.

Staring out of the window he sees Cilla pulling at a tree root, getting nowhere, but she's not giving up. Neither will he. His religion is one of joy. Light overcomes darkness. Joy in God's love can overcome sorrow. It's his calling, his challenge. Make those ritual chanters sit up.

23

February 1972

Elspeth sits bolt upright in bed. That plucked, dead bird on her plate? The callous laughter of the men around her? The one, viewing her with binoculars? What does it mean? The images won't leave her. Her dreams are vibrating at the bottom of her spine. The gun. Is it still there?

She grabs her tartan woolly dressing gown, wrapping it tightly around her. A fiery pink glow from the morning sun covers the valley, the elm trees stark in contrast. Looking at the trees again, she can make out roosting crows.

Elspeth shivers. Why has she come out without her scarf? The trees are still dripping from the early morning rain. The leather of her shoes is wet through. She pulls one off; her foot is bright red, blood-red. She recoils at the thought. Pushing her foot back in, she continues down the grassy path to the dry-stone wall. The moss on the stones is soggy, her hands muddy, as she pulls one aside to feel behind it. She's aware of her chest moving rapidly. Her fingers reassure her. She calms; it is there. Deep breaths. All is as good as it can be.

She eats lunch in the dining room, alone. She presumes Angus is too busy to join her.

Afterwards, passing the door to the Robinsons' suite, she overhears Gertrude telling Clive that she, Elspeth, has "gone do-lally." She staggers, her legs weak. Was she seen wandering? Now, lying on her bed, she realises that she does need help. But from whom? She cannot burden the family with the truth. Katrina suggested she did more yoga meditation, focusing on objects, giving them full attention.

Elspeth picks up the teak dish they brought back from Burma, runs her hand over it, feeling the grain. She sits cross-legged on the floor, the bowl in front of her. She cannot concentrate. Once she had a faith. She thought she could rely on God. Now she does not know what to believe. Will it help if she prays? Will the apparition leave her alone? Pulling on her coat, she sets off for the church.

Treading softly down the aisle, Elspeth sits in her pew, Charles' pew, and bows her head. Why did you take him? Cruel. Not loving. Tears splash onto her folded hands; she's shaking, sobbing, gulping for air.

Something comes across her back, clutches her left shoulder.

'Go away!' She turns, shoving, sees the slight body falling, hears shrieking, a clattering, followed by moaning. A grey-haired woman is lying over the back of the opposite pew, clutching her wrist. Flowers are strewn all around. Another woman, holding a full water jug, is staring with mouth wide open. A third woman puts down the tulips she's carrying and helps the older one to her feet. Heart pounding, arms flailing, Elspeth runs back down the aisle.

She stands in the church porch, wiping the tears from her face, she blows her nose, screws up her handkerchief. The tears continue to flow, she starts walking, can't see where she's going. What a fool she's been, but it is not her fault. That woman shouldn't have touched her. She stumbles over a gravestone, stops herself from falling. She stands still and breathes deeply. A dog is barking somewhere. She doesn't want to meet anyone. Tying her scarf around her head, she tells herself to soldier on.

The hill seems steeper than usual. She pauses for breath and begins to sob again. She watches starlings stalking on the grass beside her, searching for worms. She will feel better if she has a quick drink. She sets off purposefully.

Reaching the Hall, she lets herself in as quietly as she can. Angus is coming down the stairs.

'Ma, what's wrong? What's happened?'

'Nothing. I'm all right.'

He can hear the catch in her voice and watches her hurry up the stairs. He sighs. What can he do to help if she won't talk to him?

She goes straight to her room and takes the bottle of gin from her drawer, tips it to her lips, puts the cap back on and slips it into her bag before quickly making her way to the sitting room to find some orange to put with it. She is sipping the comforting liquid when she hears Angus approaching. Rapidly draining her glass, she pushes the bottle under a cushion as he enters the room.

He lifts the cushion, grabbing the bottle. 'Ma. You are *not* ok.'

She stands looking at him, blinking. 'I've had a shock. I was attacked in church.'

'He frowns. Attacked in church? I think you must be drinking too much.' He puts the bottle on the table, glares at her and strides out.

Elspeth pours another drink.

Gertrude opens the door and ushers Simon in. She's tight-lipped, but her eyes seem to be flashing a message. He follows her into the empty sitting room, removes his coat, placing it on a chair. It's the first time he's had to deal with a scuffle in church. This job certainly isn't dull.

She turns her attention to a fire burning in the grate; she leans down to the irons, selects the poker and lets the air in between the coals. The fire crackles, flames spurt, leaping higher giving the oak-panelled walls a glow.

'I'm very glad you're here. She needs help. I'll go and find her.'

He looks out at the parkland stretching away into the distance. Money and land are responsibilities he would not want. He steps closer to the hearth, his outstretched hands absorbing the warmth from the burning coals.

He turns around as Elspeth enters the room, a glassy-eyed look on her face. Has she been drowning her sorrows? Was she sober yesterday? The flower-ladies didn't mention alcohol.

'I'm so pleased to see you rector. Most kind of you to call. How can I help?'

'Lady Fairweather, I've come to reassure you that, as far as Mrs Jones is concerned, the misunderstanding has been settled. She says she scared you, made the mistake of coming up behind you.'

Elspeth knows that she has had more to drink than is wise. She focuses on Simon's face with its rosy cheeks, his uneven teeth, his neck red where his collar rubs.

'The ladies want me to give their apologies and best wishes. They realise how insensitive they have been.'

She remembers to smile, tries to take in what he's saying.

Gertrude brings in the tea on a tray, dainty china, beautifully arranged on a damask cloth.

'It is difficult for anyone to understand what you have undergone.'

‘It was frightful! They should not have touched me without asking.’ The sight of the woman sprawled across a pew comes back to her. She flops into a chair and sobs.

Simon offers her a handkerchief, something he learnt to carry with him soon after he was ordained.

She swallows and waves it away.

Elspeth smiles, reaches for the decanter and, hand shaking, adds a little whisky to her cup. ‘Rector?’

‘Thank you.’

Walking home, he wonders whether he should have refused the alcohol.

Claire turns towards him as he comes in the back door, ‘It’s good that you’re here, the meal is ready.’

‘Lovely. Some food will be good; I’ve been drinking with Lady F.’

She frowns, then realises he’s probably exaggerating the amount he’s had. ‘Gin and tonic?’

‘A drop of whisky in my tea, though I did wonder afterwards whether I should have refused. I don’t want to encourage her. I really don’t know what we're going to do with Elspeth. She needs more help than I realised.’

He pours the gravy on his dinner, watching it make a pool in his Yorkshire pudding.

‘I wonder if she would talk to you. I found it difficult.’ Simon pauses, a Brussels sprout on his fork. ‘She was too upset and had been tippling quite a bit.’

‘I have attempted to talk with her at the Mothers’ Union meetings but she’s always busy telling people about Buddhism or something.’

‘Can you have another go?’

Claire looks at him, grimacing.

‘If you could get a feeling of her mood, it might help me to find a way forward.’

24

Angus grins at Toby, poking him in the ribs. 'Welcome to success! I knew you wouldn't be able to resist the challenge.'

'Didn't have a lot of choice, did I?'

'You can tell yourself that if it makes you feel better, but you can't fool me.'

'Ok, so maybe I just want to make sure your venture has the best chance.'

'Come on, I'll show you around. You've arrived in time to go to our first race meeting at Chepstow.'

Hebrew, waiting patiently in his stall, moves towards him, anxious to be outside. Angus strokes the soft nose, looks into the brown eyes.

A feeling of accord is transmitted from one to the other as Angus canters him down towards the river. He stops abruptly; a dog is bounding towards them.

'Spike, here!' calls Claire. The dog obeys, and she clips the lead on.

He slows Hebrew to a walk.

'I'm so glad I've seen you. I've been thinking about your mother. Have you any idea how I can help?'

Angus raises his eyebrows. 'We're going to Chepstow races. Do you fancy coming? Mother would be pleased to have some company.'

'I haven't been racing for years.' She smiles. 'Yes. I'd like that.'

'Great.' Ma will be out of his hair; he can concentrate on the job. 'I'll be in touch,' he nudges Hebrew on.

25

Angus' breath clouds before him as he walks quickly to the stables. Toby has backed up the horse-box ready for Hebrew to enter. Rodney is still putting in fresh straw.

'Have you nearly finished? We need to get going.'

Rodney frowns at the harsh tone. 'Just need to fetch the tack,' he mutters.

'It's time we got Hebrew in.'

He takes the bridle. Hebrew stands his ground. Toby, coming up from behind, gently strokes Hebrew's flanks and leads him into the box.

A low winter sun shines as Angus pulls out of the driveway, following the horsebox along the winding road.

'I'm putting my shirt on Hebrew,' Elspeth declares.

'But he hasn't raced for ages, Mother, not since Brotherton.'

'I'm sure he'll do well. I'm going to back him, too,' says Claire.

'I hope you're right, we need a win, although that's a lot to ask of Rodney. He's been good in training.'

Driving into the owners' car park, Angus' pulse is racing at his first visit as a fully paid-up member of the Jockey Club. He hopes that today will be the success he needs, proof that their training is effective.

Angus helps Toby to settle Hebrew after his journey, while Rodney makes his way to the weighing room, seeming more relaxed now that he's beginning his task.

Elspeth climbs out of the car quickly, looking around at the opposition. It's always interesting to get inside other groups and see the types of people and feel their energy, just like the audience watching when she and Charles had gone to the theatre. They'd loved it, it was part of the entertainment.

Her gut clenches, she moves away from the memory. She's surprised to see such a variety of cars and people. Angus has parked alongside a vintage Bentley: a large ruddy-faced man in a tweed suit and a cloth cap easing himself out of the driving seat; she wonders which horse he owns. On his other side, a slim young man with long dark hair is taking coats out of the boot of a Ford Escort. She watches as he carefully assists a very pregnant woman to get out of the car and helps her on with her coat. The older man is barking at his wife, who is limping around the bonnet of their car.

'Hurry up! We need to find the others.'

Elspeth wistfully thinks of Charles. He would have been holding her coat for her, taking care of her as much as she would have allowed. She sometimes wishes that she hadn't been quite so independent. She wants cherishing now. Why had she not allowed it before?

The older couple move to where a group of people are gathering, with much shaking of hands and kissing. It looks like a special occasion for them. The young couple make their way carefully towards the main stand.

She needs a race programme so that she can select her horses.

'Come along, Claire,' she says, spotting mulled wine at the bar, 'I think we need to lubricate our luck. Drinks first and then we can decide on our bets.'

Angus sighs. Was it a good idea to bring her? He'd thought that it might brighten her up but perhaps it's tipping the balance too far. He wonders how much help Claire is going to be as he watches them, wine in hand, giggling over their selections.

As the final race begins, the sun disappears behind a cloud, a cold breeze blows. Rodney gets Hebrew off to a good start, jumping well. Elspeth, waving her racecard enthusiastically, cheers him on loudly.

Angus stands firmly, his binoculars trained on the pack, watching closely. 'He's clearing the fences well.'

Toby yells, 'Come on Rodney, you can do it, only three more!'

The commentator is shouting too. 'And Hebrew's in the lead going into the last, with Shapeshifter making up ground, oh, a slight stumble by Hebrew, and

Shapeshifter is closing the gap, and Shapeshifter wins, followed by…'

Angus lowers his binoculars. 'Well, that was bloody disappointing. Thought he had it in the bag. What on earth was Rodney thinking of at the last fence?'

'God knows!'

'That's it then,' says Angus. 'So near and yet so far. Maybe we'll have more luck in the flat season when we've got a professional jockey.'

26

March 1972

In the Blacksmiths Arms, Geraint chomps on his sandwich, spilling bits of cheese and onion. He's on a fool's errand. It isn't as if he didn't make an appointment; he's done everything Rodney has told him to do.

Maybe the woman got it wrong, and Angus is still waiting for him somewhere in that rambling estate. If only Rodney had been there. The Fairweathers have got money, new stables, the chance to get known.

He slurps his beer. Money means they can get a top jockey. He wishes Angus hadn't been so encouraging on the phone instead of telling him straight there was no chance of a ride. But perhaps there is, perhaps he's mistaken the date. No point in driving this far to give up too easily. When did the woman say Angus would be back? Early afternoon. Give it a bit longer, let Angus eat in peace and then go again. At any rate the sandwich is fresh, and the beer good. Can he allow himself another half? Better not. Might give the wrong impression.

He looks up as a middle-aged man in a blazer and sharply creased trousers comes in and starts talking to the barmaid.

Leaving the pub, Geraint wanders down to the river; it is full after the previous day's rain, sparkling golden in the cold air and sunshine. He relaxes into the stillness around him, standing on the old stone bridge, barely wide enough to take two lanes of modern traffic. A lone fisherman casts his line, waits a few moments, eyes on the water, then reels it in, and prepares to cast again.

Geraint turns towards the noise of a car engine, the blue Rover from the pub yard approaches, almost brushing against him as it crosses the bridge, goes past the church with the low tower and further up the road heads into the Fairweather estate.

Elspeth puts the last answer into the crossword as Gertrude clears the dishes away. The afternoon stretches ahead. What to do? She pulls on her shoes and heads into the park, the cool breeze on her face, refreshing. Walking briskly, she's aware of her energy returning.

In the orchard, she slows her pace, sees new buds opening, touches the trees, feels the living bark.

The sound of a car travelling up the drive seeps into her consciousness; it stops, a car door closes. She opens her eyes; a man is heading towards her. The scream surprises her. She backs away, panting, clinging to trees, he's getting nearer.

'Elspeth,' he calls, 'It's me!'

The voice is one she knows.

'Elspeth!'

'Huw!'

She freezes, sees him standing with arms outstretched towards her.

'Remember I came to see you in Istanbul.'

She lets go of the tree, steadies herself, raises her eyes, looks above him, sees small white blossoms, purity.

His oversoft voice grates on her ears.

'I thought that we had a special connection and that you thought so too.'

She drops her gaze. The perfume of his after-shave strikes her. She'd allowed him to embrace her, found his warmth strangely comforting, his masculinity attractive. Why has he not been in touch?

'Elspeth, I've been thinking about you for some months.'

She gives a quick shake of her head.

'Can I offer you a cup of tea?'

'Thank you, but no. I think it's better if we take a stroll and have a chat.'

Her eyes narrow; her body tenses.

'We must be careful where we meet; if the press knows you're seeing someone, it could add to your problems.'

Angus is driving through the mountains in good time for his appointment with the bank manager. Things should go well. After all, the family is highly respected and has been using the same bank for over fifty years.

In Brecon it is market day, and the streets are busy. There is a parking space outside the bank, a brick building from the turn of the century. Walking through the tall wooden doors, he holds his briefcase containing the papers he has spent hours on; the costings for the work, the running expenses, suggested prices for more horses.

A young woman greets him, ushers him into the manager's office. To his surprise he doesn't recognise the man. He looks an austere fellow, thin, with half-moon glasses, perched on a narrow nose. When he speaks, his voice is surprisingly deep.

Angus takes out his papers and begins to explain.

The bank manager remains silent until he's finished examining the papers.

'Hmm. It's all a bit of a gamble, isn't it?'

'No, I don't think so. It's all costed.'

'Ah, but with the current economic climate, I doubt it will be as you've forecast. Head Office won't approve this.'

Angus frowns at him. Why can't the short-sighted old fellow see that Whistledon Stables will be a real money-spinner in a few years?

'Perhaps you'd like to keep the budget forecast and run over it again.'

Passing the documents back, the man gazes at him, his lips unmoving.

Angus sighs, he won't be so unadventurous when he reaches this chap's age. He's worked and worked with Rodney to keep the costs down; it's not really an option to sell off any land. The farms are profitable and employ local people. The Hall needs modernising, but he's avoiding spending money on that. He's working for almost no income, and poor old Toby is doing the same. It's a good job that he's footloose and fancy free with no one depending upon him.

Turning into the drive, he sees a blue Rover parked on the grass verge. There's nobody in sight. Glancing in the rear-view mirror, he spots his mother stumbling out of the trees. He stops, climbs out, shouting,

'Are you all right, Ma?'

'I'm having a walk.'

Simultaneously, a man appears, hurrying in the opposite direction, slips into the Rover, turns it around and heads for the main road.

Angus stands his ground.

'Mother. What on earth is going on? Who was that?' He looks at her more carefully: she's upset, distressed even. 'Come on, Ma, tell me all about it. Who was it and what did he want?'

She shrugs. 'He's the man the Foreign Office sent to Istanbul. He called in to see if I'm all right.'

Angus puts his hands on his hips. 'What? After all this time, he turns up unannounced, scares you and asks if you're all right? There's something wrong there.'

She covers her ears with her hands. 'Please don't shout.'

Dropping an arm around her shoulders, he smiles. 'Sorry. People should leave you alone.'

'He said he's been thinking about me. I'm not sure about him. I know too much about how the F.O. works. He brought back memories.'

Angus looks at the forlorn woman that she's become. He hadn't realised how much she has changed in the last few weeks. He's neglected her since she's been back, his mind and energy focused on the stables. 'I think you'd better get in the car; I'm not having them bothering you like this. You must let me know if he contacts you again. I'll have him stopped.'

'No, no! I don't want any fuss.'

'He needs reporting'.

'It's my fault. I should have recognised him straight away. I don't want to get tangled up with the F.O.'

'He should have made an appointment. It won't do.'

'I'm sorry I allowed him to upset me. He said he'd come to help.'

Angus glowers, 'We don't need help from him. It's the bank manager who should be helping. He'll regret it one day, when we're up and running properly.' He shifts in his seat. 'It was a new chap I saw this morning. I'll show the short-sighted blighter. It's ready money we need. The man has no idea about horse racing.'

Elspeth sighs.

'I was wondering if we could sell the statue. It must be worth quite a bit.'

She sits back; eyes open wide. 'No. No,'

Helping her out of the car, he can see her body shaking. Her face is taut, her lips pinched.

'No worries, Ma, there are other banks.' He guides her through the front door.

'I think I'll lie down.'

He watches as she slowly climbs the stairs.

'The jockey is here.' Gertrude appears in the hallway. 'I've shown him into the library.'

He smiles his thanks and makes his way to find Geraint, who is gazing at the Stubbs prints on the walls.

'Impressive.'

'Geraint. Thanks for coming. I'm looking to have some racehorses worthy of their places on walls.'

'Rodney tells me it is an exciting new venture. You will need a good jockey.'

'He tells me that you might be the one.'

'I would very much like to be'.

'Did Rodney explain that we're at the very beginning of the venture?'

'I understand you're looking to develop a training business.'

'That's right. Come on, I'll show you around. You can meet the horses.'

Angus is pleased the likeable young man is willing to accept reasonable terms and grow with the stables.

As Geraint drives away, Angus remembers he needs to call Dominic about the man in the Rover.

Elspeth wonders at the feeling in her gut. Is it fear or excitement? She wishes that she had been more welcoming. If only Huw hadn't surprised her, shocked her. Pictures of Istanbul flash in and out of her mind. There was no one else she could talk to; everyone else was too afraid of upsetting her. Her first image of him: the trim figure in the smart blazer and tie, taking her by surprise.

Later, how he held her close to comfort her, the strength in his arms. Memories crowd into her head; the journey they had taken across the Bosphorus, to visit the palace and gardens, on the Asian side of the city. It was a day of respite. He had wanted somewhere away from all the fuss in the consulate. His hand holding her arm as they stood at the bow of the boat. Seagulls swooping around the little boy eating his sandwich. She could hear their screeching and the cries of the boy.

Huw had walked with her through little streets where shopkeepers called to them. Over the last year, she has thought of him, of their meetings, his eyes undressing her, his gentle touch, at first comforting, but which became firmer and firmer, almost intimate. The comfort he'd given her was somehow wrong. It excited her; she's becoming aroused at the thought. He appeared very circumspect, but she felt his desire. She was numb with shock, her emotions awry.

Now she has over-reacted; he's frightened her into letting him see how vulnerable she is still, and alerted Angus into being overprotective. He doesn't need her to add to his problems. She must sort herself out. Perhaps Huw has come at the right time, but she must be careful where and when they meet; she's a free agent. Angus won't like it, especially if the news gets around.

Driving back to St Asaph, Huw mulls over how foolish he's been. He'll look ridiculous in Angus' eyes, for that's who it was; he heard him call her 'Ma'. Has he lost his touch? She was more disturbed than he expected, she was very withdrawn, welcomed him as a friend at least, but wasn't very forthcoming when he asked questions. She seemed nervous, kept looking about. Did she think somebody was watching her? Is she afraid of Angus? She'd always spoken fondly of him. Is he bullying her?

What does she know about any subterfuge? Is Angus involved? Was Charles shot because of it? He needs to keep in touch. He must write to repair the damage.

Back in his lodgings, Huw looks in the mirror; his forehead is more lined than he realised.

27

Angus puts the accounts to one side. He'll have a walk down to the Blacksmiths Arms for a pint; the fresh air might clear his head and help him find a way forward.

He won't invite Rodney or Toby to join him. He needs to concentrate. He'd been so anxious to see the bank manager that he'd clean forgotten Geraint Adams' appointment. It was a good job that the jockey had persisted. They need to be creative, find different ways of funding the project.

First though, he'll go round the stalls and check all is well. It's been a strange day, his plans for the bank loan thwarted, and then that creepy fellow arriving, upsetting Ma. She'd said he was interested to see horses. Why? No business of his, F.O. or not. Pa had always been careful to keep them at arm's length.

Arriving at the Blacksmiths Arms, he's surprised to find Toby and Rodney already there; he's forgotten it's darts night. They're both enthusiastic members of the team. He buys his pint and sits down to watch but can't stop thinking about the way the man from the F.O. accosted and upset Ma. Is he on a mission connected with Pa and the gelding? He needs to keep Ma away from him. She's suffered enough without being involved in a scandal. Better be on his guard, destroy the letters. But Blast! Bank transactions can be traced. Banks are a flaming curse.

The game is soon over with the Blacksmiths Arms the winners. He buys the team a round, and leaves, trudging through the clinging mist, unable to shake off his anxiety.

Some hours later, he wakes with a start, he can hear horses' hooves. He peers out. He can't see any movement. All is still. He must have been dreaming; but he stays leaning against the windowsill, narrowing his eyes, staring into the darkness. Is the F.O. watching the estate, do they have the details, know what they're looking for? How can he explain the horse's absence from his stables? They would find it easy to prove he'd exported it. Oh God, he was beginning to understand why Ma was so uptight. Was Pa's reputation about to be ruined? The whole Fairweather baronetcy to go down the tubes?'

28

Claire opens the porch door, letting the dogs inside, taking off their leads and dropping a towel over each one before it can shake and spray the walls with mud. She can hear Dinah talking with Simon on the other side of the kitchen door. 'Will one of you give me a hand please?'

Simon squeezes into the porch, grabs Spike and begins towelling him down.

'Paw,' says Claire to Cilla, wiping the pad underneath. 'The canon was in the woods. Spike dashed off barking ferociously; he really doesn't like him.'

'You ought not to let him do that, he'll give someone a heart attack.'

'Difficult to stop when he's off the lead. Besides it's a rare occurrence, part of his job of protecting me.'

'I'm all for that.' He kisses her as she opens the door, all four of them going through to the kitchen.

Claire removes her wet macintosh. Simon holds it at arm's length as he takes it to drip on to the tiles in the hall.

‘Well, what was that all about?’ she says, looking at Dinah as he returns. ‘You sounded to be having a good discussion’.

‘We’ve been discussing Paganism. I’ve been invited to take Matthew to stay in Oxford for a couple of nights for Ostara, that’s the Spring Equinox, you know.’

‘I didn’t know, but I have heard about some strange Pagan rituals at Stonehenge. I’m not sure that’s a good idea. There will be more talk than ever.’ She turns to Simon who is listening with an amused look on his face.

‘I’ve told her she should go! We are all better for some spirituality and it doesn’t have to be Christian. Certainly not with the outdated rules that run our churches.’

Claire takes a deep breath. ‘You’re the one who will get the flak from the Parochial Church Council.’

‘I’m going to meet them head-on before they can start their complaining. Dinah’s got a good idea for a social evening in the church hall. We’re going to have a slide show with tea and cake.’

‘About Paganism?’ Claire wrinkles her brow.

He laughs. ‘No. “A Celebration of All Things Bright and Beautiful”. Of course, Paganism isn’t excluded, so if anyone wants to submit photos of woodland ceremonies, and other such happenings, I’ll be delighted to receive them.’

‘You won’t get any from me, Dad. I don’t possess a camera.’

Claire and Simon wave as Dinah leaves with her friends. Matthew is crying as he lies in his carrycot. Dinah, next to him, is stroking his head. The couple in the front of the car, her friends, are smiling and waving too.

‘He'll soon stop and drop off to sleep with the car's motion.’ says Claire.

‘I suppose so.’ Simon is feeling surprisingly bereft as they leave. He gives a big sigh. ‘I’d better get on with Dinah's idea.’

‘Who would have thought you would be taking suggestions from a Pagan?’

‘I'm not sure the archbishop would approve, but I'm sure Dominic is broad-minded enough to see the sense of it.’

Claire pats his arm. ‘I do think it will go down well with quite a lot of people, although you may get some holiday snaps.’

‘All things bright and beautiful should include holidays, but I’m expecting more.’

‘Yes, it’s a good wide topic.’

‘I’ll get my camera; it'll be pleased to have an outing.’

In the study, he reaches on the top shelf for his camera bag. Pulling it down he rubs the dust off with his sleeve.

‘I’m going to potter into the woods; see if I can get some good close-ups to get people guessing. Make them think.’

Claire grins, ‘That could be dangerous.’

'It's no good going on as I am. Dinosaurs, men on the moon and we still churn out the centuries-old words. It's no wonder we are losing members.'

Creativity is what he needs. The afternoon is fine; there is a little warmth in the sun. He trudges through the dense, damp foliage, humming to himself. He nods as he clicks the shutter, capturing a spider on its web, raindrops sparkling.

Claire heads into the garden; the pillowcases are hanging limply on the line; a waste of time putting them out. The familiar sound of a tractor brings comforting images of childhood, cycling along narrow country lanes. Farmers are always busy. She has things to do, but none of them bring the joy that Dinah and Matthew kindled.

Half-an-hour later, the herb bed is free from weeds; she stands with a satisfied sigh. Dinah will be happy introducing Matthew to her friends.

The choir is in good form today. Simon sings softly as he makes his way to the pulpit, climbs the steps and turns to look down on the sea of faces. It is a good day; the church is half-full. As he begins his sermon, he senses people sitting up, listening with interest as he talks about Dinah and his photographic excursion.

'As many of you know, my daughter has chosen the Pagan way of life. I was at first disappointed that she was making the decision to step away from the Church of England. Now, having spent time learning about Pagan beliefs, I find that I can understand Dinah's reasons for taking a different path. We should not let our beliefs divide us. We need to look for common ground. God's handiwork in nature should be a good start. I'm suggesting an evening sharing slides, photos taken by anyone from Whistledon, in celebration of it. I look forward to receiving contributions as soon as possible.

29

Elspeth puts aside her book; she is not following the thread. Istanbul is all she can think about. Angus was right, that man should not have come. As he turned to hurry away, he said, 'I'll be in touch.' What did that mean? He finds her attractive. She can see his eyes; his gaze holding hers.

A walk down to put some fresh flowers on Charles' grave will bring her back down to earth.

Passing through the hallway, she pauses to pick up the post, three letters addressed to Angus and one to her. It has a St Asaph postmark. She carries it back to her room, takes the paper knife and slits the envelope.

Her hands are trembling, gripping the letter.

St Asaph

Dear Elspeth,

It was lovely to see you, though I must say, I wish I had not alarmed you. Next time, my dear, I shall be more considerate.

I'm happy to tell you that we won't have long to wait for our next meeting. I'll be living quite near you, very soon, in a cottage by the river. I'm looking forward to spending time exploring the area. If you will accompany me that will be wonderful.

I shall be at the bridge on the edge of the wood at 11 o'clock this Thursday morning.

Yours in friendship,

Huw

Is this what he meant? Angus won't be pleased. She studies the neat, bold handwriting: nothing like Charles' free-flowing script. Is she being rash? It will be good to have someone else to talk to, someone to distract her. He knows how awful it was in Istanbul. He comforted her. She misses Charles; sometimes she wakes in the middle of the night thinking that he is holding her. He has gone. She must make a new life for herself. Forget the old Elspeth. She is still here and needs to get on with her life.

She puts the letter down on her dressing table, looks at herself in the full-length mirror. Smiling, she sits in her chair, closes her eyes, relaxing. Thoughts of Huw tantalise her. "A special connection," he'd written. She's ready to discover more about him, indulge in physical pleasures... perhaps.

What would Charles think? What would he expect her to do? He would want her to be happy. He would understand that she needed the company of a man.

First, she will put some flowers on his grave. Let him know he isn't forgotten, let the villagers know he

isn't forgotten.

Elspeth is too wide awake; she can't rid herself of the disturbing images. Huw in the Grand Bazaar. A totally different look on his face; it is not kind. He is always smiling when he is with her. Who would he have been buying jewellery for? Is she being foolish meeting him? Does he want her to confide in him? Tell him what? Is she under suspicion? No, it must be Charles they are investigating; he wasn't happy, was he? Had he given secrets away to that young woman? Do they know about the horse and the statue?

She swings her legs out of bed, stands, clenching and unclenching her fists. She pulls back the curtains. There has been early morning rain. Dark clouds are drifting across the hilltops. The grass in the valley is as green as ever. Elspeth watches as the sky over the most distant hill lightens. She must not shrink from life's challenges. She will meet Huw.

As she walks across the paddock and down towards the river, she can see that the clouds are becoming lighter, the sky is brighter. She can't forget the way he looked at her. What does Huw want from her? Why do they think she needs more counselling? Has Angus told someone she is disturbed? If only they would leave her alone. The river is full, low branches dragging in the water.

Walking along the muddy riverside path, she nears the bridge. Huw is not there. A lone coot is bobbing along with the current. She isn't going to stand about waiting. She turns and follows the little black bird as it sails downstream. Suddenly, she is aware of footsteps behind her, pacing softly, steadily. She freezes.

Footsteps...

'Charles! Stop! Listen!' she can't hear anything but the ferry crossing the Bosphorus. She looks behind her. There is a man. Charles crumples to the ground beside her, she can see the hole in his shirt and the blood beginning to seep through, she sinks to her knees. 'Charles!'

A firm hand on her shoulder brings her back to the present. 'Elspeth, I am so pleased to see you.'

Charles, no, not Charles. Huw.

He smiles, taking her wrist.

'I'm sorry if I startled you again. This is why you need me to help you.'

Elspeth sighs, perhaps she does. He moves his hand, stroking her arm, his touch is soothing. She breathes in deeply and relaxes, sees the calm river, the mud under her feet. Pushing away memories of the vast expanse of water, the baked earth, the blood, she allows him to lead her towards the edge of the wood, where the path is wide enough for two. The robin singing in a bush, the sound of hooves cantering across the grass, Huw steering her towards an old oak tree. She trembles, he leans her against the rough bark, stands in front, facing her.

'Sometimes, my dear, physical pleasure can heal the deepest wounds.'

Elspeth stands, closes her eyes and allows the gentle hands to ruffle her hair, to massage her shoulders, to open her coat and fondle her breasts. His fingers trace her nipples; she gives a gasp of pleasure and relief. The feeling is short-lived; they can hear the slow clip-clop of a horse, being walked along the river path.

Elspeth pushes Huw away. 'I think you'd better go. I don't want people talking.'

Huw quickly takes a pamphlet out of his pocket, presses it into her hand. 'Have a look at this; we could get to know each other properly.'

Elspeth puts it into her pocket, shuts her eyes, 'I will read it later. Please go now.'

Huw turns and hurries through the trees towards the bridge.

Elspeth stands listening to the sound of twigs crackling under Huw's feet. Imagines his neat, shiny shoes stepping carefully between the brambles. She heaves a sigh of relief as they gradually become fainter until they disappear altogether. Then she leans back against the sturdy oak and sobs. What is she doing? Her legs are weak, her lower body aches, she doesn't know what she wants. She opens her eyes, sees the budding branches, the river beyond the trees. Slowly, she makes her way towards the river, stumbling over brambles and tree roots. She pulls the pamphlet out of her pocket, reads "St Bueno's Jesuit Spirituality Centre". Dominic won't like that. Stuffing it away, she watches the river lapping gently against the path; she could just keep walking and wash away her turmoil. She closes her eyes again, listens to her innermost thoughts. How can she live like this?

'Ma, are you ok?' Angus is astride Hebrew, walking back along the river path.

She pulls her coat around her, smooths her hair. 'Yes, yes, of course I am.'

Angus dismounts, frowning, 'why don't you walk up with me. I'm going back to the stables, and we can have a drink.'

Elspeth is quiet as they cross the park.

The stable door is open. Rodney is there, rubbing Jericho down.

He twists around to look at her; 'Ma, do you want to give Rodney a hand?'

Elspeth takes the offered brush and begins working on the sweating flank, the rhythm of the strokes calming her. The horse stands quietly until Toby clatters in with Greg.

'Did you enjoy the walk with your friend?'

'Not a friend. Just someone I met.' She turns back to her task.

30

Rain is rattling on the conservatory roof. Angus lowers himself into a chair opposite to where Elspeth is sitting staring out at the sodden grass. Anger seeps through him as he replays yesterday's disastrous scene. He swallows his anger down. He understands she finds the horses soothing, but she can't keep unsettling them by popping up in the stables whenever she feels like it. Percy Adworth had come early in his van, to prepare Hebrew for the Chepstow races, but when Rodney took him to the stall, they heard Hebrew whinnying and found Elspeth standing in the corner. Hebrew immediately shied. The farrier asked that he be left alone with the horse to try and calm him down.

Despite his best efforts, he was unable to shoe him. Percy said that in his opinion, even if he could get the plates on the horse, it was inadvisable to put him through the stress of the journey.

Rodney thought that was good advice. He pointed out that Percy is very experienced in dealing with thoroughbreds; he is used to their temperamental behaviour.

Angus watches the water gathering in a pool on the patio. Drip, drip, drip, he's gradually drowning in all his problems.

'Ma, I don't know what's going on with you. Rodney said Hebrew was in a real state yesterday. Why were you in his stall?'

Elspeth is unable to speak. She doesn't know. Why did she go to the stables? She can't remember. Perhaps it was because she'd had that dream. It was a frightening dream about being on a horse that was careering away with her; she was clinging to his back. She must have wanted to see the horses were calm and all right, but then they weren't. She didn't expect them to react to her in that way. She had looked in at Jericho first and then Hebrew. He had reared up and whinnied as if he had seen the ghost. She hadn't even had the time to close the door before Rodney had arrived. She hadn't done anything to disturb Hebrew; she wouldn't do that.

'Rodney was hoping to make up for his lack of success in February.'

'I know. I was looking forward to cheering him on.'

Angus shakes his head

31

Upper Whistledon Hall

My dear Huw,

I'm intrigued by your suggestion. I'm not sure about a Jesuit retreat. I was talking to my daughter, Katrina, about it when she came at the weekend (I didn't mention you, but I showed her the leaflet.) She pulled a face and suggested I ought to think about going to a Buddhist centre, instead. I agree with her. That would be so much more me. I've practised yoga for years; I have always found the meditations very helpful. It all started when we were posted to Burma and were having a particularly torrid time. It's good that it's becoming more available here. I don't expect you, in your position, would feel able to come with me on a BUDDHIST retreat. I'm thinking of going anyway. I'm surprised that you were suggesting a JESUIT one. As Katrina says, 'Only God can forgive.'

We had a lovely weekend; she has two children and brought their dogs too., so there was a lot of walking, running about and chatter. Quite exhausting, although we did get some respite when Angus and Toby took the children to meet the horses. I'm rambling on so will stop.

I look forward to being with you again soon. We must find some way to be away from all the prying eyes. I, too, do not wish to make our relationship (if I may call it that) public yet. I do feel rather confused. I know that I am a single person, but I had not expected to meet anyone who would awaken desire again. I'm afraid that we were seen in the woods by Toby. He did not know who I was talking to, but another visit here is unadvisable.

I wait to hear from you in the hope that we can find some way of being together again.

Yours,

Elspeth

Willow Cottage

River Lane

Whistledon-on-Wye

March 1972

My dear Elspeth,

I am disappointed to hear that your family have such sway over you. I thought you an independent spirit. Our families don't know what's best for us. Only we know where our destiny lies. We need to find a way to be together. I am wondering if you remember the Daltons from Buenos Aires. They have offered me the use of their cottage in Llanarch. There is no need for anyone to know the Daltons won't be there.

I hope you think this an excellent idea.

I shall book the cottage as soon as you let me know the best dates for you.

Yours in anticipation,

Huw

Upper Whistledon Hall

My dear Huw,

I remember the Daltons well. How did you get to know that I was friendly with Sue Dalton in Argentina? A lovely couple, we still exchange Christmas cards. I'm very tempted by your invitation. I know that I am a free agent, but it is hard to go against people who obviously care for you. On the other hand, I know that they want me to be happy. I will just say that I am going to stay at the Dalton's cottage.

I think that spending some time together will be exciting for both of us. I have very little in my diary at the moment, but I have been asked to help with the flowers for Easter Sunday. I had a little difficulty with some of the flower ladies recently and this is a reconciliation exercise. I would like to be back here on Good Friday ready to fulfil my duty. Or we could go immediately after Easter. I am sure that you must be busier than I am and probably have Easter duties.

I look forward to hearing from you.

Yours in excitement,

Elspeth

Willow Cottage

River Lane

My dear Elspeth,

It is wonderful that you are going to join me in the Dalton's cottage. It is in a very tranquil area. I think we should go as soon as possible, say this coming Saturday? I'll stock up on the essential foods before you arrive.

If this is too soon, I will simply re-arrange.

Longing to hear from you,

Huw

32

Hebrew clears the recently raised practice fence with ease. Angus sighs with satisfaction. It's a good day. Mother's off to stay with friends, people who will give her company and support; getting away from Whistledon, from memories, will give her a chance to recover. A break for him too, from the totally unpredictable behaviour, from skirting around conversations, treading on eggshells.

Elspeth watches Clive lift her suitcase into the car boot and gives him the calmest smile she can manage. Careful Elspeth, she thinks. She must not look too excited. She is just going to stay with a friend for a week. The fact that the friend is Huw must not be known. Memories of Huw caressing her, are sending electric shocks down to the base of her spine.

She smiles again at Clive, thanks him and slides into the driving seat. Her body relaxes as she drives along the tree lined village road. She's escaped, is free from the over careful attention of Gertrude, Angus too. It is bad enough being bothered by an apparition, without everyone being overly concerned about her welfare. Huw is interested in her for herself. He tells her that she is an extremely attractive woman, he knows the attraction is mutual.

Llanarch

Huw is at the cottage before her; there are flowers on the kitchen table. Looking into her eyes, he pulls her towards him. She presses against his body.

'Now, I have you. A whole week to discover each other.' Stepping back, he kisses her lightly on the cheek.

She turns and views the room; it seems comfortable enough. 'There's a piano in the living room. How unusual but then Gordon does like his music.'

'I can knock out a tune. Enjoyed playing for the troops.'

She walks to the window and gazes out over fields, hills in the distance. It is extremely isolated.

'Our nearest neighbours are a pony-trekking place, about a mile away. We shouldn't be disturbed.'

She hopes she hasn't been rash. No, Huw is a clergyman. 'I'd like to go pony-trekking.'

'We can do that.' He raises his eyebrows, smiling.

'Oh, Huw, it's so good to get away. I drove here in quite a blur, feeling lightheaded because I wasn't having to control myself all the time. You are very kind to me, it's wonderful that you've managed to arrange this so quickly.'

'Come and have a look at your room.'

Elspeth smiles, this is something she's been concerned about.

'If you don't mind, I'll make a cup of tea and have a wee dram just to settle me down, bring me back to earth. It all feels like a dream.'

Huw leaps across to the kettle and switches it on. 'I've got a tray ready with bara brith and look here's a bottle of Macallan. I thought we'd both love that.'

She laughs. 'Oh Huw, I can see that we're going to have a good week.'

He opens a cupboard door and displays a wine-rack. 'The Daltons say, "Help yourselves." They want to do anything they can. When I was talking to her, Sue said, "There, but for the grace of God, go I."'

Elspeth smiles wanly, 'How extremely thoughtful. I suppose I am seen as a bit of a victim now. Come on, the kettle is singing.'

'I'll get the whisky.' Pouring it into her tea, he says, 'Have you brought your walking boots?'

'I have.'

'That's good, we can go walking tomorrow, when we've had a good night's sleep.'

Elspeth sits by the stream, Huw stretched out, eyes closed, beside her. Mesmerised, she watches the water rushing down the hillside, careering around boulders and fallen branches. Travelling miles through fields and villages until it's lost in the salty estuary. She looks down at Huw, gently touches his arm. He smiles, sits up, rests his hand upon her knee. The light touch sends shivers up and down her legs. It's all part of a game. She knows he can feel her desire; her breathing gives her away. Elspeth, calm, slow and deep breaths. His hand gently moves up her thigh. She can stand it no longer. She turns to him, her lips seeking his. He draws her towards him. Pushing him away, she stands, picks up the rucksack, passes it to Huw.

'Not now Huw, we have a hill to climb.'

He holds out his hand for her to pull him up, clasps his arms around her, whispers in her ear, 'Wait till I get you home, you little witch.'

Elspeth shudders, remembering Charles calling her that before they were married. She breaks free and sets off, stepping out as much as she can.

Huw catches her up as she stops for breath.

He pauses with her to gaze out across the hills. The countryside is bathed in sunshine; sheep are grazing in the fields. The path is following the stream, now narrower, a raven pecking at the edges. The large black bird senses them watching and flaps away. The path is becoming steeper and rockier. She stumbles. Huw catches her arm, 'Steady Elspeth. Take it slowly. Don't want any mishaps, do we,' supporting her as she searches for a foothold.

He is right; she must tread more carefully. She's intent on reaching the top. Her thighs and calves ache. They will be tired after this unusual exercise. She should sleep well tonight. The journey downhill is equally demanding, and her knees are aching.

Elspeth is pleased when they turn into the lane to the cottage. Huw has been quiet. Is he exhausted too? Is she being disloyal to Charles? No, she's made her decision, needs to go ahead, it's what she wants.

Huw pours two glasses of wine and sits on the sofa. ‘Do come and relax, my dear.’

She sits next to him and rests into his shoulder.

Elspeth turns on the shower, allowing the warm water to envelop her. She’s very aware of her body. Her back arches as she breathes in deeply, remembers how she responded to Huw’s touch. She smiles at the thought. Stretching her arms, she lathers them, then her breasts, body and thighs. She’s pleased she’s taken care of herself, is still desirable. A pang of guilt as she thinks of Charles; it passes quickly, he hadn’t appreciated her fully for some years. This morning she’s happy to be alive. She surprises herself when she hears her voice singing.

Huw lying in bed calls, ‘I think we should ask the Daltons if we can stay another week.’

‘I wish we could, but I have promised to do the Easter Sunday flowers.’

‘Someone else can do those.’

‘No.’ Elspeth is very torn. Wanting this delight to go on forever. Huw has awoken a primal desire. She sighs, almost content. Underneath she knows it's really Charles that she wants beside her. Life is cruel. That young woman, who inveigled Charles, must know it too. The thought changes her mood. ‘No, Huw, we need to pack and go home today.’

33

Whistledon on Wye

March 1972

Simon sets up the projector on the high table, lines it up carefully with the screen that Claire is manipulating into position. This idea seems to have struck a chord with some of the non-attending villagers. The church needs people. It is a beautiful building, a stopping place for walking groups and some cyclists, but not many come in to pray; although it has a definite atmosphere which quietens even the loudest of the groups when they get inside.

Auntie Vi had been very impressed with the energies she could feel. There was a lot of love, she said, but there had been great suffering too at times. To be expected with its age.

He looks at the slide he's using as a guide. Sharpens the focus slightly. He's pleased with the detail that he's managed to capture.

Claire comes across. 'That's good. You are clever. You have always had a good eye.'

By his side are three boxes of slides from the amateur photographers of the village: sunsets, close-ups of flowers, and a variety of landscapes. He also has several named envelopes containing one or two slides; as expected, these are posed shots of young family members, sometimes with their pet animal. Overall, they show what an attractive village Whistledon is; could be good publicity for the few B&B's. He hopes no one will be upset that he has weeded out their slides; the ones that did not seem to be in focus when he ran them through his handheld viewer.

He strides to the door, welcoming people.

'There will be tea and coffee afterwards, if you would like to stay for a chat.'

The fifty folding chairs are nearly all occupied when he starts the show promptly at seven-thirty with a photo of the Blacksmiths Arms taken by the landlord. Simon smiles as cheers erupt. He imagines some would rather be going there for a pint than staying here for a coffee.

He gasps as a photo of the bridge appears on the screen. There is more in the picture than he realised; on the small viewer he saw beautiful reflections of the arches in the river. Now he can see two people on the footpath: Elspeth Fairweather and Canon Lloyd. He clicks to the next one, wondering if anyone else noticed the canon's arm around her. What is going on between them? Concentrating on the slideshow, he puts them to the back of his mind.

34

Upper Whistledon Hall

April 1972

My dear Huw,

I must thank you for that splendid holiday. It was all I dreamed and more. I do hope that you found it as fulfilling as I did. I found more contentment on the hill walks than I have had for a long time. It was good to go pony-trekking. The evenings sitting on the sofa, chatting, and getting to know each other – I quiver at the memory.

My dearest Huw, I do hope that we can find more time to be together. I do need you. My problems seem to crowd around me when I am alone here.

I could imagine that I am with you. Otherwise, I will lie on my bed and remember.

With love,

Elspeth

Cathedral Close

St Asaph

April 1972

Ma Cherie,

I am desolate that I was unable to be with you for your celebration. Life without you is miserable. I long to feel your touch, your body next to mine. I shall be in Saint Amand in a few weeks, ready for our new life together.

Je t'envoie cent bisous.

Ton mari aimant,

Huw

Willow Cottage

River Lane

April 1972

My dear Elspeth,

It was splendid indeed to spend time with you. I'm already planning our next holiday. Can I drive you to Cornwall or Devon in June or July?

You are always in my thoughts.

Love,

Huw

Upper Whistledon Hall

April 1972

My dear Huw,

It would be wonderful to be in Cornwall. I know of a cottage in Rock where we can stay. It is very discreet. Excitement rises as I write.

Katrina is encouraging me to go on a Buddhist retreat; it appeals to me. I hope to hear from you soon. I will find out when the cottage is available for us. I do long to have you close to me again.

With love,

Elspeth

Willow Cottage

River Lane

April 1972

My dearest Elspeth,

I am most excited at the thought of spending another week with you, this time in Rock. Shall we say the first week in June?

On Friday I am going to walk over the hill to Nether Whistledon. I'll be at the stand of beech trees by 11 o'clock. Are you able to join me? My darling, we must enjoy these fleeting moments until we are away together again.

Your Huw

Upper Whistledon Hall

April 1972

My dear Huw,

I am sure that you saw me ride past this morning. I was very frustrated. Toby rode up behind me. I dare not stop. I was just getting near the copse when I heard the hooves. It's been over a week since we were together. Angus keeps asking me questions about where I have been and who I have seen. I must start to become less predictable. Perhaps on Monday we should meet in the afternoon. In the same place at 2:30. Will that be all right for you? I will be there regardless.

Love,

Elspeth

35

Elspeth canters Ezra across the grass down to the riverside path. Huw will be waiting for her. She reigns the pony in to take the path carefully; his chestnut coat is shining, his dark tail swishing, Elspeth is happier than she's been for some time.

Passing near to Willow Cottage, she thinks Huw will be walking to the stand of beech trees. She must let him get there before her or they might be seen together. How frustrating it is to be hiding their relationship. Or, she wonders, does it give her extra excitement?

She slows Ezra down to a walking pace as they climb the hill. he takes it in his stride. She leans forward and pats his neck.

The beech trees come into sight. Is Huw there? He'll be keeping a low profile, waiting behind a tree. As she nears, she gazes eagerly, the only movements made by some crows, pecking at a small carcass on the grass. They fly away as she approaches. All is still. There's no one there. Leaning forward she caresses Ezra again, feeling the warmth of his body. The warmth she wants from Huw.

Her heart sinks as she sees, coming from behind the second tree, a tall figure in white, a ghostly spectre, gazing at her. He turns and walks away.

The strength drains out of her legs and arms. She drops onto Ezra's neck. Why does this keep happening? What can she do to stop it? Where's Huw? Ezra seems to understand. She turns him around and makes her way back towards the village.

Elspeth puts Ezra's bridle over his head thoughtfully. Where is she going to ride? Where might she find Huw? She passed by the beech trees a couple of times on Tuesday, hoping he might be there. On Wednesday, she walked into the village. His car was not outside Willow Cottage. She returned on Thursday. His dustbin was not out. Where is he? Where has he gone? It is ridiculous behaving like this, she tells herself, but she is becoming very upset. He isn't here to soothe her. distract her from the repetitive images of Istanbul.

Waking up in the night, she tossed and turned, went downstairs, made herself a cup of tea, tried to read a book, got out her Bible. Her head is aching, her temples throbbing. This can't go on. She sobs inwardly. She must get out of here, get away from everyone and then she might escape the torment.

Reaching the stable block, she can hear Toby in the next stall talking to Jericho. She must go. Quickly, she mounts Ezra and sets off to cross the grass down to the riverside path.

She needs to check the wall. No, she mustn't do that. It's better to let grass cover the path she's making. Ezra tosses his head. Elspeth takes a deep breath. She must calm herself; Ezra is picking up on her desperation. She pulls him to a halt and gets off. She'll walk for a while. It is no good. She stands, leaning against his flanks sobbing uncontrollably. Thank goodness there's nobody to see her.

36

Arriving back at the Hall there's a letter on the side table. Huw's writing with a French stamp. She picks it up and, trembling uncontrollably, quickly makes her way up to her bedroom.

Why has he gone to France? And without telling her. She knows that they have no real ties, but they have been so close. Their intimacy deserves more than this. The floor seems to be shaking beneath her feet. She must lie down. She can hear Gertrude coming up the stairs, then tapping at the door.

'Can I bring you up a cup of tea, Lady Fairweather?'

'No, no, go away. I'm having a rest. Why are you disturbing me? Leave me alone. Why can't people just leave me alone?'

Logis des Halles

Perigueux

My dear Elspeth,

You will be surprised to see a French stamp on this letter. I'm so sorry I could not let you know that I wasn't able to meet you. I am travelling all over to find a cathedral town to twin with St. Asaph's. I can't wait to hold you close. I will be back in Wales in two weeks' time.

Yours ever,

Huw

Two weeks. She needs him to hold her hand, to stroke her hair and make her feel safe.

She hears Gertrude's footsteps retreating down the stairs. She has two weeks to live through without falling apart. Slowly, she gets to her feet and crosses over to the rosewood writing desk. She puts the letter away and then reaches into the drawer to find her whisky flask. She pours a measure into a glass. Two weeks. She must make a plan; do something to fill the time.

She looks out of the window; Ezra is grazing in the paddock. Her gaze travels beyond, to the pasture where the sheep have their heads down, eating; all they do is eat and sleep. The time will pass more quickly if she's asleep.

She tops up the whisky in her glass. The smell has a calming effect. She sips, feeling it burn its way down her throat then warm its way through her chest. Enough of this will make it easier to sleep. But waking up with a whisky headache will be even more painful than it is now with gunshot sounds ringing in her head

She puts the glass down, opens her desk, flicking through the stack of papers, until she finds a letter from Katrina. She has sent details of a Buddhist retreat, perhaps she is right to suggest she spends time connecting with herself. She will do that. Charles would never have expected her to mope around for two weeks simply waiting for him. She certainly isn't going to do that for Huw.

37

May 1972

Angus drives away with a lightened heart. He hopes this week will be a real turning point for her. The last few weeks have been very trying. He desperately needs the horses to settle down. The way Hebrew was so freaked that Percy couldn't plate him for Chepstow was a real shock to Rodney, and very disturbing to himself. There must be changes.

Maybe Ma will have to get professional help, or go back to Scotland, if Robbie will have her. The project will founder altogether if the horses are too disturbed to race.

The thought of the stables failing is not to be contemplated. He could sell the farm, but it would be the thin end of the wedge: he wants to improve his inheritance, not watch its demise.

Rhyader

The garden rooms are attractive. Well-fitted-out with everything for comfort. Elspeth had worried about being trapped in a small white cell but, whilst being very simply furnished, the accommodation is welcoming. A smiling Buddha is stationed at her door. She sits on the single bed with its white counterpane. It feels firm, but soft enough. She bounces up and down a few times, then gets to her feet and views the garden. It is surrounded by a picket fence. She can see two women hoeing. They're talking as they go; one occasionally stops, bends down to examine a plant. and then continues. An old chap in overalls is leaning on his spade, lighting a cigarette.

Normal life goes on. Her frantic mind and frenzied action seem far away, but she still lives with it. Perhaps here, she can become her old self again. No, she needs to accept change. She needs to learn to live with her conscience or whatever it is, that's driving her to distraction.

She picks up her case and placing it on the bed opens it. There's a small wardrobe; carefully, she hangs her dresses and trousers on the hangers. Lies on the bed, staring at the ceiling. She's startled by a tapping on the door.

'Time to come and have a welcome cup of tea.' says a soft voice.

She smiles at the robed grey-haired woman, who leads her slowly to an airy room, with chairs arranged in a circle. People are already seated. She takes the offered cup of tea and sits in one of the few remaining places, between a long-haired young man and a morose-looking woman. She focuses on drinking the hot sweet liquid until the circle is complete when a yellow-robed monk waves his arms to encompass everyone. 'I'm very pleased to welcome you all to this sacred space. Let us introduce ourselves. First names only and you can choose your own. I am Reuben.'

Elspeth straightens. Who shall she be?

He continues, 'Sometimes a new name can find a hidden part of us. Help to drop an overactive ego.'

Elspeth feels his kind eyes upon her. Is she showing her distress?

'There is no right or wrong, just different; we accept each other as we are.'

He pauses.

She looks around at the others, a young woman, twisting a ring on her little finger, a bearded man next to her shuffling his feet. There's an old fellow. Could he be the one who was smoking in the garden? His face is very craggy; he must be at least eighty. A woman leans to her neighbour and whispers in her ear. The leading monk watching, says nothing.

Elspeth tenses, is this a confessional? She must not let her guard down.

'Would you like to start? Please add a brief description of what you hope to gain from this retreat'.

The quiet-voiced monk is addressing the young woman. The girl blinks and looks around the circle.

'My name is Joy,' she says. 'I want to learn how to escape from the noise and bustle of the world.'

'Pearl.' The name drops easily from Elspeth's lips. It feels good to cast off her identity. 'I, too, am seeking inner peace.' Several heads nod.

The introductions over, the monk gently strikes a Tibetan singing bowl.

'To complete this opening session, we will chant the mantra Om Mani Padme Hum. Please join in. Just give yourself permission to enter the spirit of the occasion.'

The chanting is still ringing in Elspeth's ears as she makes her way back to her room. She had forgotten how much of a release Buddhist chanting can be. It's at least ten years since she has been in such a group

Selecting a mat from the shelf, Elspeth looks for a space. The room is almost full. She is surprised to see the craggy old man sitting cross-legged on a mat at the front. She would prefer not to be in the direct view of the leader; it is a long time since she practised yoga. She selects a place near the back, lies down and closes her eyes. She can hear chattering; she doesn't want to talk. She has come here to try to sort herself out, not to be distracted by others.

A gentle chime stills the voices. She hears the request 'Please lie down, close your eyes and listen to your breathing.' She feels a sense of relief as the energy in the room changes. Moving through the postures, she wonders why she hasn't persevered with this before.

Afterwards, feeling a sense of calm and wellbeing, she decides that she will keep up the practice when she goes home. She has been at the beck and call of men for too long. She needs to love and look after herself. Huw has betrayed her. Charles did too although that was different. Charles was part of her real life. Huw is just part of the nightmare that has overtaken her. He was extremely attentive at first when he'd flown out to help her, but then he had disappeared for all the time that she was in Scotland, only to suddenly arrive in the orchard at Whistledon that day, and now where is he? She has become over-reliant on him.

Four days of living in a community where she is constantly being reminded to be in the moment, to do everything in a mindful way, is beginning to change her thinking patterns. She can see how frantic she has become. A feeling of strength courses through her. She is going to become strong and independent again.

38

Whistledon on Wye

Elspeth runs her fingers over the little jade Buddha, feeling the curves in the stone, before putting it back onto the windowsill. It had been a surprising, but very thoughtful gift from Gertrude, when she had arrived back from the retreat last week. She knows that she is much calmer than before she went there. Life is getting better. The sun is shining,

She will saddle Ezra and hack around the parkland, take the path away from the village. New mindful beginnings mean making deliberate choices.

She rides for an-hour-and-a half in a big circle before the Hall comes back into sight, the mellow stone glowing in the sunshine. They pick their way carefully across the stable yard where Angus and Rodney are stacking posts for a new jump to be installed in the training paddock. She unsaddles Ezra and gives him a rub down, mindfully maintaining the bond between them. It's a beautiful day. She's enjoying each activity as she thinks about her actions. Finally, she leads Ezra back into the main paddock to join the other horses.

Closing the gates with a satisfying click, she takes a deep breath of fresh country air, and feeling the ground beneath each step, returns to the Hall for lunch.

'Hi Ma, it's good to see you looking more cheerful.' Angus opens the door to the dining room, letting her go ahead.

'I do feel much better. Katrina was right, a retreat was just what I needed.'

Angus grinned, 'You can always count on Katrina.'

'The meditations were a challenge, but I worked through them, and it was lovely to potter about in the garden.'

'I'm sure we can find you some weeding if you would like.'

'Then I had forgotten how powerful yoga is. Have you ever tried it? I'm sure you would find it useful.'

'I'll bear that in mind. I've a lot to do just now.'

Elspeth smiles, knowing he has absolutely no intention of trying it.

Elspeth looks at the carrots in the dish that Gertrude has put onto the table. Her mind is back in the garden of the Retreat, holding the bright-orange roots by their feathery green fronds. Gratitude, mindful gratitude is what she must hold on to.

Angus unfolds his napkin. 'I saw Claire yesterday; she reminded me that the church Garden Party is next month.'

Elspeth raises her eyebrows. 'What are you doing for it?'

‘Oh, no, she is wondering if you will still be organising the flower-ladies stall.’

‘Of course. I told her I will. It’s not like Claire to forget.’

‘I think she is worried that your Buddhist interests might mean you are turning away from the church.’

‘Silly woman. Buddhism enhances Christianity. She should know that.’

‘Glad to hear it.’ He adds a helping of broccoli to the omelette on his plate.

Gertrude has put the Parish Magazine on the side table too. It’s open at the page advertising the Church Garden Party. She must remember that she needs to be of service as part of her commitment to her spiritual development. It will be her pleasure to assist the flower-ladies.

39

Huw pours himself a beer and finds some crackers and cheese, takes them out to the small table in front of the kitchen window. The grass, grown tall whilst he's been away, stands still in the evening sunshine; mowing must wait until tomorrow. His need for neatness is sometimes a worry. Monique panders to it to some extent. It was wonderful to be back with her, to feel the warmth and satisfaction of their loving, to eat her delicious meals. She is a casual and relaxed woman, unlike uptight Elspeth who is extremely alluring but not an easy nut to crack.

Finishing his supper, he clears away then strolls around the garden in the gathering dusk, before locking the doors and climbing the stairs to bed.

As he lies there, he can see the polestar through the window. He and Monique had seen a sky full of stars from the patio of their cottage. They had looked at the polestar last night and thought about his journey north. He wonders if she is looking at it now and thinking of him. He's tired of living in Whistledon, it's a lonely life. Tomorrow he will cut the lawn and write to Elspeth. He's aware that her stress heightens his own, increasing his need for order. The letter can wait.

40

June 1972

Claire goes to her drawer and fishes out last year's journal.

Simon raises his eyebrows, 'I thought you said you were happy with the arrangements?'

She smiles. 'Just checking, I want to be sure everything runs smoothly.'

She looks at the notes in her hand, compares them with those in her book. 'Hoopla, skittles, kick the football, guess how many biscuits in the jar; they always keep the kids happy, and some of the parents too.' She runs her eyes down the list, gives a satisfied nod.

'Then, this year there will be silk flowers to buy, and of course cakes and buns and strawberries and cream. I'm going to be helping on the teas again.'

Leaning over Simon, she gives him an encouraging kiss on his cheek. 'All the stalls are allocated. You won't have to do anything but walk around smiling.'

He takes the list from her. 'Thank you, darling. The forecast is for a dry day. Let's hope it's right. It's never the same in the church hall.' He smiles wryly 'This year we have the added pressure of Elspeth's attendance.'

He rolls his eyes. 'She'd better not start handing out leaflets on Buddhism.'

Dominic, driving along the country lanes to Whistledon, has a feeling of relaxation. It's good to be able to visit Elspeth and Angus and combine it with a visit to one of the churches in his diocese. He enjoys being part of parish life, able to support garden parties, without the responsibility of arranging them. His presence will be appreciated by some of the congregation.

He recalls his time as a vicar with the pressure of encouraging his faithful flock to raise the necessary money to run the parish. Dwindling church attendance is evident everywhere. When the clergy connect with the local community, then hope springs.

He was on the panel which appointed Simon, remembers being impressed by his desire to help all members of his parish, whether they attend church or not.

Dominic turns into the drive of the Fairweather estate and continues up the hill to the Hall. Elspeth is looking out, ready to greet him.

Together, they walk to the rectory gardens, to join the volunteers setting out their stalls. The lawn is a hive of activity; trestle tables are being decorated with coloured crepe paper, balloons inflated with helium, labels prepared ready to add the sender's identity.

The flower-ladies are eager to seek Elspeth's advice and Dominic leaves her, making his way over to a group of older people, who are sitting chatting and watching the activity; the old stalwarts of church Garden Parties, the ones who crocheted doilies, baked and sold cakes, ran tombolas and generally oiled the wheels of the fundraising waggon. Now they're sitting back and enjoying the company.

Simon hears the laughter coming from the group, sees Dominic's ready smile. If he'd known earlier that he'd be spending the weekend with the Fairweathers, he would have asked Dominic to say a few words. He switches on the microphone to test it. Before he can speak, Dinah appears, talking excitedly.

'This is Jack from New Zealand. He says he's your son.'

There's a gasp, a momentary hush, as the assembled company take in the words issuing from the loudspeakers. Dinah is smiling from ear to ear. The tall young man standing next to her looks anxious.

'My mother's name is Abbi. Do you remember her?'

Simon drops the microphone with a clatter. Who? What? Why hadn't she told him? Taking a step forward, he smiles broadly, grasps the young man's shoulders and, looking at him intently, nods again, taking both of his hands.

Elspeth, arranging silk flowers in a vase, pauses and sees a younger version of Simon, about the same height but slimmer. She turns back to the table, stands erect, looks at the other helpers and determinedly picks up another flower. She is firmly in charge; the less fuss made the better.

Claire, in the middle of serving tea, stands poised, milk jug in hand. Her heart is thumping. This can't be true. It must be some sort of stunt. But why? Simon seems to be taking it seriously. She watches him go into the house with the young man and Dinah. She feels stupid, left out, as though she's being fooled. She senses eyes on her, smiles and puts the milk jug down, empties a packet of biscuits onto a plate.

She swallows hard, wants to know more, to go indoors but she's determined to keep behaving as if everything is happening normally.

The hubbub dies down; people are back at the stalls. A burst of laughter erupts. Is it aimed at her?

Dominic stands before her, cup and saucer in hand. 'You're doing a wonderful job, Claire. There's nothing like a cup of tea in the afternoon to settle the mind. Would you pour me another please?'

'My pleasure Bishop.'

'Perhaps I can stay here while you go in and see what's happening.'

'Would you? Thank you. I'm sure he can't really be Simon's son; he's so against premarital sex. I'd better help him sort things out.' Claire puts the teapot down firmly. 'Thank you so much. I need to make sure that everything is as it seems. I'm sorry to say that not all people can be trusted. Simon always sees the best in people.' Hurrying into the house she finds Dinah and Simon sitting talking animatedly with the young man around the kitchen table. He has in his hand a silver chain with a silver heart on it. 'My mother says you gave this to her.'

'I did.'

Claire looks up at him. He returns her gaze

'Claire darling meet Jack.' She raises her eyebrows 'Can I have a word in private?'

Elspeth leaves the ladies to finish clearing the stall and count the takings. It has been a very interesting afternoon; she doesn't join in the chatter about the rector. Generally, the remarks are kind, but it has certainly sparked gossip. She looks for Dominic; he has been wonderfully calm all afternoon. Now, he is nowhere to be seen. She supposes that he is talking to Simon. She walks back up to the Hall alone, smiling to herself.

Going into his study, Simon opens the safe and locks the cash away. The takings are up on last year's. It has been a great day, he has an inner joy, knowing that he's fathered a son. In fact, he's elated; he can't describe his feelings in any other terms. Maybe he should feel embarrassed and ashamed, but he doesn't. Somehow, having a son gives him more kudos in the parish. He didn't always live by society's rules and Jack is the proof. It is as though his inner rebel has been acknowledged. Dinah seems delighted to have a half-brother. There is a knock on his door, Dominic peers in, eyebrows raised.

Outside in the garden, Claire is working off her anger, vigorously collapsing tables. So that's where Dinah gets her morals from. Here she is being Mrs Rector, an unpaid slave of the Church, behaving with propriety, when Simon is swanning about, so proud of his immoral act. She grunts at the verger as he carries the last table away.

Without guile, totally open and straightforward, that is Simon, or that's what she had thought. But now...? Her world has been turned upside down; the ground seems unstable. This Simon is unknown, not simply a bit different but nothing like the one she thought she knew. How could he do this to her?

Dominic is just leaving to walk to the Hall. He gives her a sympathetic smile. 'How are you, my dear?'

'Her eyes flash. It's not every day you find your husband has an illegitimate son.'

'It was during the war; life was precarious.'

'Does that excuse his behaviour?'

He pats her on the shoulder. 'We are all fallible. Bless you, my dear. Thank you for all your hard work.'

She is not sure that she is ready to go inside. She stands, looks at the trampled grass, it will soon recover. She must give him a chance. How many years of experience is there between that man and this? Nearly thirty; what was she like at that young age? Naïve but not stupid. Men are expected to be more adventurous than women. She has never known the Simon that fathered Jack. Her Simon is a different man. What is he thinking now? Especially after the way he has treated Dinah.

Her reaction has been too hasty. She has a stepson and needs to welcome him to the family. Heaving a sigh, she goes towards the house to talk to Simon.

She finds Simon sitting in his chair in the study, a stupid grin on his face, and can't resist a dig.

'I don't know where this leaves you,' she hisses. 'All that high moral tone you've been taking with Dinah seems almost laughable. It would be if the whole village wasn't tutting about you.'

Simon stands up, opens his arms and embraces her. 'My love, I didn't know. I'd almost forgotten about her. My first experience, long before I knew you.'

Claire sighs. 'He seems a very pleasant young man. Dinah's taken him for a walk by the river with Matthew. I suppose I'd better find some sheets and make up the spare bed.'

The early morning sun is shining through a chink in the curtains. Simon lies, eyes closed, remembering yesterday, his body is suffused with a warm glow. He pictures the young man who is now sleeping in the spare room. He looks at Claire, his excitement tinged with sorrow. How she would have liked a son. He's going to have to reassure her, help her bear the memory of the unborn child that had died in her womb.

She will love Jack as she loves him, he hopes. Dinah seemed excited; she had always wanted a brother. He wonders about his position in the parish. The church wardens will be having another meeting about this. He knows which ones will be supporting him.

The bed creaks as Simon eases himself out; He pads across the room to the chair and pulls on his dressing gown.

Downstairs, he lets the dogs out into the garden and fills the kettle for an early morning cuppa. He shakes his head as he reflects on Jack's arrival. What an introduction to the parish. He pours the boiling water into the teapot and leaves it to mash while he fetches a bottle of milk from the fridge, adding some to his cup. He gazes out of the window at the clear blue sky, pleased the weather is fine for Jack's visit.

He thinks back to Abbi. Why had she kept the secret all these years? Why hadn't she told him? It was great she'd told Jack when he'd asked. Simon thought about the paternity test that Angus had taken. Did he want one? No. Jack was only here for a couple of days and then going to work in London looking after the homeless. Thank you, God, for bringing my son to Britain. His gain was Abbi's loss. He realises he needs to get on and write today's sermon. Carrying his tea, he heads to his study.

His aim is always to respond to situations, to find the right text for the moment. He picks up his Bible, sits holding it between his hands. He takes his notebook from the shelf. Opens it at the next clean page. He lays it on his desk and selects a pen from the pot at his side. He needs the ink to flow freely. He closes his eyes, asking for guidance.

His mind needs quietening; he must find the place of stillness within himself. He can see the faces looking at him, looking away, then returning surreptitiously to watch his reactions. He can see the shock on Claire's face. Last night she pointed out very forcibly that his attitude to Dinah must be giving him cause for thought, saying, “Sometimes chickens come home to roost.” He’s pleased that he’s married to Claire. How would he feel if she’d given birth before they’d met? Would he have accepted the fact, the child, or would he have turned away from her? He shrugs; he loves her.

The congregation is more of a problem; this isn’t what they expect from him, the man who preaches the sanctity of marriage. What sort of example is he setting for the youngsters? He needs to be open about the situation, ask for forgiveness. It was a youthful careless moment that created Jack. His sermon will be on tolerance and everlasting mercy. He begins to write, putting down his thoughts as they arise. He will include the hymn, “Dear Lord and Father of mankind, forgive our foolish ways”.

He’s singing as he strides out into the herb garden, wanting to talk with Claire before the service. He sees Jack, looks at his son with love and pride; a son who has new-world ideas of tolerance, ideals which chime well with his own. Next to him is Claire, bending down, listening to him as she picks parsley.

'I'm wondering whether you'll be coming to the service this morning,' Simon looks from one to the other.

'I was just saying to Claire, that I'd like to take the opportunity to hear you preach.'

'And I was saying it would be good to show a united front, but only if that's what you'd like.'

'It is. That's settled then. My sermon, and my life, are in God's hands.'

Jack frowns. 'I was taught we have free will.'

'It's ok, I take full responsibility, but trust in his guidance. I may have been foolish, but my only regret is that I didn't know about you earlier.'

Claire looks up at him. 'Would it be awful of me to say that I'm pleased you didn't?'

Jack grins. 'I have had a very good life so far, so there's no need for self-flagellation. In fact, once my parents knew I had decided to come to England, they expected me to contact you, if I could. I've always known that Dad isn't my real father. He thinks it's important for people to know their backgrounds.'

Simon flinches at Jack's mention of Dad but quickly accepts he has no right to expect such a reference for himself. He wonders how Jack would have turned out if they had known each other. Would his son have become a Pagan too? What religion does he have?

41

Simon looks across the table at Claire. 'Dominic is coming for a cup of tea. He has a proposition for me.'

'A proposition? What sort of proposition? Is he bothered about the family morals? Perhaps he wants us to move where nobody knows us.'

'We shall see. He's staying at the Hall, so will be here soon.'

'I like it here. I don't really want to pack up and go somewhere else. Angus has invited me to the races again.'

'That is kind of him. Though I expect he's hoping you'll keep Elspeth under control.'

Claire laughs. 'She's more likely to lead me astray.'

Simon smiles as he gets up to answer the doorbell.

Dominic is in one of his more sombre moods. He accepts Claire's offer of a cup of tea, and while she disappears to the kitchen, he looks Simon in the eyes. 'I'm sorry to have to tell you that there have been rumblings; some of the churchwardens are unhappy with your leadership. They feel you are a bad example, even question your faith. They worry that others will follow your lead,' He waits for Simon's response.

He nods his head but says nothing.

'They say you are condoning the Free Love Movement. Ignoring the Church's teachings about the sanctity of marriage.'

'I don't know how they can accuse me of that when Claire and I have been faithfully married for over twenty-five years.'

'It was the appearance of your son that sparked the unease. I know that doesn't really make sense but...' Dominic shrugs his shoulders.

'If someone is intent on pointing the finger, I guess they will use the flimsiest of reasons.'

'Unfortunately, they were already unhappy that your daughter has a child out of wedlock, and when Claire took him to the Mothers' Union, that, as one of them said, "rubbed salt in the wounds". I can only say I thought you both behaved compassionately in the circumstances.'

Simon breathes deeply. 'I preach God is love. They obviously are too bigoted to listen.'

'I know this isn't the easiest of places to work; you have faced some extraordinary challenges. Lady Fairweather and I appreciate your fortitude.'

Simon rubs his neck.

'In view of this we are most determined to keep you. That's if you want to stay, of course. Lady Fairweather was telling me how hard you and Claire work.'

The rattling of teacups announces Claire's return. She sets the tray on the table and pours.

Dominic continues, 'She was telling me too that she is grateful that you allow yoga classes in the church hall. Many clergy are afraid of losing their power if they recognise another religion, not that yoga is a religion; however, it does have spiritual associations.'

Simon's shoulders relax.

Dominic turns to include Claire in the conversation. 'It was whilst I was speaking with Lady Fairweather, that I was reminded of a young man who is almost ready for a parish of his own. She was explaining her interest in Buddhism. I know that Kris Lewis has made a special study of other religions to find the common threads with Christianity.'

Simon raises his eyebrows. 'That is something I have been thinking about, particularly since Dinah challenged me by becoming a Pagan.'

'It occurred to me that this would be a placement where he could use his knowledge to good effect. I'm sure that you would find him of great assistance at this time.'

'You can be sure we will make him very welcome. We look forward to his company, don't we Claire?'

Claire smiles broadly at the bishop. 'Of course. There's always more than enough to do.'

Dominic smiles his support. 'Change is needed if the Church is going to survive.'

42

Angus has a quick breakfast, smiling confidently at Gertrude as he pushes back his chair, taking the £5 she wants him to bet on Gregorian Chants.

He crosses the stable yard with long strides, eager to set off. Whistledon Stables are going to be tested again. Rodney and Toby are encouraging Greg into the horsebox. They've prepared him well, his muscles quivering with stored energy, his grey coat shining. Jericho, already inside, whinnies and clatters his hooves. Rodney, the most experienced, seems very calm; he is the one who has pushed the decision to enter this meeting.

Angus stands watching, hopeful. The horses have worked well in their training, their times improving steadily. With only a few horses, it is easy to keep an eye on them. There will be more pressure when they have clients. He mustn't allow himself to become overwhelmed by it all.

Once safely installed, with Rodney in the driving seat, Angus takes the Land Rover out of the garage ready to follow.

He looks towards the house, Where's Ma? She said she'd like to come with us. Perhaps she's changed her mind. The horsebox is already on its way down the drive; he can't be hanging about. She'll have to miss out. Suddenly she appears, almost running out of the front door. Clutching her handbag and breathing heavily, she climbs in beside him.

In the parade ring, Angus watches Rodney leading Gregorian Chants around, bridle grasped firmly. Rodney is ready for it; able to control the horse as he shies at noises coming from the crowd.

Angus turns his attention to Geraint, resplendent in the distinctive Whistledon colours of purple and silver. 'Give him his head. Once he's on the track, he'll settle down. Just doesn't like waiting around. Good luck.' He stands back as Rodney gives the jockey a leg up. Time to find Toby.

He is by the on-course bookies' stands, putting a betting slip into his wallet, and grins at Angus, 'Nothing ventured, nothing won.'

'I hope you haven't overdone it. I was tempted. I'm hoping for some prize money too. The sooner we start winning, the sooner owners will bring their horses for training.' We need a steady income. He turns and makes his way slowly back to his mother, suddenly aware of the tension in his neck. Is she right, has he over-stepped his limits? His diminishing assets, the bank manager's doubtful expression flick into his mind.

What would Pa have said? A surge of annoyance sweeps over him. He knows he is taking risks, but he *does* know what he is doing.

Toby is walking briskly to collect his winnings. Geraint has performed as well as can be expected, riding Jericho into fourth place in a big field, with Gregorian Chants, unplaced, uncomfortable with the soft going. Gertrude will be made up with her each-way bet and the return on her fiver. Ma needs watching; she's has had a little too much bubbly, laughing and joking.

'It's worth a celebration,' she says. 'Gertrude will be pleased. I'm sure she will be happy to make a meal for Toby and Rodney too.'

Toby shares out the last of the wine in the bottle he brought with him. 'That didn't last long. Shall I go and find another? He turns to Angus. I can nip down into the cellar. I'm sure there's something there that will make you feel more hopeful.' He smiles broadly.

'Be careful', warns Angus, 'the stone stairs are very worn and uneven; there's a light switch on the right.'

Standing at the head of the cellar steps, Toby, looking into the pitch-black space, fumbles for the switch, negotiates the steps with care and enters an aisle of well-stocked racks. He hasn't been down here before. It's a different world, shows the history of wealth of this family.

He scrutinises the labels. Chateau Laffitte. That should do the trick. Picking it out, he retraces his steps. Then, about to go back up the stairs, notices a large wooden crate at the end of the rows, tucked up against the wall. What's in there? It looks as if someone has started to open it.

He puts down the bottle and peels back the protruding cardboard. His fingers touch something smooth and cold; he yanks a little more away; can see white marble. He pushes his hand down under the brown paper, traces the curves of a head, feels a little more. Are these horns? He prises away the wooden slats, then, gradually unwraps the object from its protective covering. The creature is playing a pipe. He continues to pull the stout paper away until he can clearly see a tail and strong hindquarters. It is a statue of Pan. Angus must have been too busy to unwrap it. He feels the weight, slowly lifts the heavy object out. Holding it very firmly, he carries it up the stairs, step by step, lowering it to sit by the cellar door. As soon as dinner is over, he must get Rodney to help him.

Elspeth gasps and raises her eyebrows as Toby puts the bottle on the table with a flourish. Heaves a sigh of relief as Angus says,

'No, old chap, I don't think we'll drink that tonight. I'll put it back in store tomorrow.'

Toby mumbles, 'Oh well, I suppose we've had enough. Perhaps a glass of port with the cheese.'

'Then we need to go; there are horses to look after in the morning.'

Rodney chimes in, 'Yes. It's been an excellent dinner after an excellent day. Thank you.'

'I need your help. It won't take long. This way.' Toby leads Rodney to the cellar. Wait a minute.' He goes inside then re-emerges, struggling with the statue.

'Where on earth did you find that?' Rodney gazes at the sculpture,

'In a corner, by the racks, Angus must have forgotten to put it out.'

Rodney frowns. 'Maybe he didn't like the look of it.'

'It will look great in the dried-up pond in the rose garden.' He bends his knees to take the weight. 'Come on, get hold of it.'

'You might be better off asking Angus to help you.'

Toby assesses the small-statured groom. 'You'll be fine.'

'On your head be it.' Bending, he lifts and, carefully, they carry the heavy statue along the trellised path, avoiding the straggling roses, putting it down frequently. At one of the resting spots, Toby says, 'Perhaps this isn't such a good idea.'

'We're nearly there.' Rodney isn't about to lug it back again. 'I'm sure it's around that next trellis. One last push.'

They shuffle their way past. There ahead is the empty lily pond. Heaving their burden over the wall, they gently lower Pan to stand in the centre.

‘That brightens it up,’ Toby grins. ‘Good job, well done. Angus will be impressed.’

Toby wants to wait until the exercise gallops are completed. He can’t tell Angus yet. Rodney has no such inhibitions; by the time Toby reaches the stables, Angus seems tense. Rodney, standing beside him, looks uneasy. Angus turns towards Toby as he enters.

‘We'd better get on and then you can show me. I don't think Ma is going to be very pleased.’

Angus follows Toby through the gardens. He stops. Toby turns to see a look of horror on Angus’ face.

‘What made you decide to put it there?’

Toby puts his hands in his pockets and shrugs. ‘You don't like the position?’

Angus glares at him. ‘I hope no one saw you with it. I'm not sure that's the best place for it.’ He must be careful not to make too much fuss. What to tell him?

‘Did you have somewhere else in mind?’

‘No, no.’

Toby realises Angus had no intention of displaying it. ‘Were you planning to send it somewhere?’

‘I haven't really decided what to do. The important thing is Ma mustn’t see it. No one must see it.’

‘Do you want me to put it back?’

Angus shakes his head. ‘I'll give it some thought.’

43

‘He’s very late!’ Claire picks up the blue jacket she is knitting for Matthew. ‘If I'd known he was going to be as late as this, I would have gone to the races.’

Simon, pouring himself a cup of tea, responds, ‘Frustrating for you.’

‘I do enjoy the atmosphere. It's exciting when you feel part of the team.’

‘I'm glad you stayed home and made these scones anyway.’

‘Don't eat them all. He may be here any minute.’

‘He needs to come soon; I want a curate that I can rely upon.’

Claire springs up as the phone rings. ‘Perhaps that's him. Perhaps he's lost.’

Simon, mouth full of crumbs, is happy for her to answer the call.

She is soon back. ‘No, it was Angus. They've had a good day; I think he's been celebrating. He said Elspeth missed my company.’

She bends to pick up her knitting but stops as the doorbell rings.

Standing in the porch is a young man. 'I'm Kris Lewis, later than I intended to be. I hope it's not a problem.'

'No, not at all. Claire Shorthouse.'

'I do apologise; I was waylaid by some workers picketing a building site. I spent longer talking than I realised.'

'Oh, hard to ignore. Not that I would want to.'

Simon, coming into the hallway, overhears. 'Well done. You can tell me about it over a cup of tea, then I'll show you to Primrose Villa.'

Simon is waiting again, pacing the kitchen, making the dogs restless.

Claire clips on their leads. 'Come on, let's go for a walk.'

'I need to introduce him to Elspeth. She won't hang about after she's finished doing the flowers. I don't want to go chasing after her. In fact, I'll go to the church now.'

Kris pulls clean clothes from the case open on the floor of his bedroom, dresses quickly and runs down the stairs; there's just enough time for some toast. Eating, he puts on his shoes, fastens his jacket, picks up his keys and heads to the door, avoiding the piles of books he unpacked last night.

At the thatched cottage across the road, a man wearing a dog-collar is putting a briefcase into the boot of a blue Rover. Should he stop and say hello? No, the man has not seen him. Kris turns right and hurries over the bridge towards St Peters.

Elspeth clips the stalk of the final lily and pushes it into the vase. As she steps back to check on her work, the church door opens to reveal Simon with a young man.

'Lady Fairweather, I'm so glad you're here. I'd like to introduce Kris, our new curate. He is going to be a great asset to us all. Kris has travelled a lot and is very experienced in comparative religious studies. I think you'll have much in common.'

Elspeth gazes at the young man. His slim body, his direct brown eyes, his tanned skin, his black hair. She steps forward, offering her hand. He's quick to shake it.

'Good to meet you. What a beautiful display.'

Simon nods. 'God provides colourful raw materials, and Lady Fairweather works miracles. I'll leave you two to chat.'

'The bishop wonders if I may be able to help you.'

'In what way?'

'I'm studying the supernatural.'

'Did Dominic tell you about the apparition I saw in the walled garden?'

'I should like to hear more about that. Can I call at the Hall? I have some books that might interest you.'

'By all means, do.'

'

44

It is early morning when Simon sets out to take the dogs for their walk; as he emerges from the little wood, he hears the men in the stables. Glancing to his right, he's curious to see Elspeth hurrying across the grass, away from the Hall. She pauses, looks about her, continues. He calls the dogs to heel, clips their leads on and stands still, by a gorse bush, watching.

As she reaches the drystone wall, she stops. Scanning the parkland around her, she dashes alongside the wall towards a hawthorn tree. She disappears behind it, emerging a minute later to walk directly towards the Hall. What's she doing? He waits until she disappears around the corner of the stables before moving.

He sets the dogs free and wanders across to the tree as casually as he can. An area of grass by the wall is flattened; he steps closer, a loose stone is clear to see. He pulls it out, lays it on the ground. Carefully, he puts his hand into the significant gap, almost immediately, feels something smooth and hard. He grasps the cold object, pulling it out. 'What on earth!'

He looks around, nobody in sight. Fingers shaking, he puts the gun on top of the wall whilst he replaces the stone. Why has she hidden it? What is she going to do with it? Is she going to use it on herself? He hopes it isn't loaded.

He'll have to tell her he's found it, or she might think the thief intends to use it. Should he consult Dominic, tell Angus? What to do with it? Pointing it downwards, he hurries back to the rectory, the dogs scurrying alongside.

He places the gun on the kitchen table, hangs up the leads and dithers. He should have worn gloves before handling it. Picking it up again, he takes it to his study, hides it in a drawer. Out of sight, out of mind. Is that what Elspeth is thinking?

That night, an image of the gun lying in the drawer keeps him awake; did someone see him with it? In the morning he'll phone Dominic and arrange to visit.

Hearing the urgency in Simon's voice, Dominic is a little worried. What has happened now? He hopes it's not another complaint from the churchwardens. He's already reminded them of the need for compassion.

He makes his way to the library, looking out of the window at the garden, all beautifully manicured, before taking a file from his desk, and sitting at one of the occasional tables. He busies himself making notes from the document spread out before him, until hearing the doorbell, he stands to greet the rector.

Simon, barely pausing for breath, puts his rucksack onto a chair, opens it and pulls something from the main compartment. Dominic's eyes widen; he holds his breath as Simon unfolds the blue hand towel that he's taken out. Wrapped carefully in the middle is the small, neat revolver.

'I didn't want to go to the police.'

'Where did that come from?'

'I found it in a wall on the Fairweather estate. I think I saw Lady Fairweather hiding it.'

Dominic gasps. 'I see. It looks like one that might be handed out to diplomats for self-defence.'

'I was worried that Lady Fairweather might use it on herself, she's been very disturbed lately.'

Dominic looks him in the eyes. 'Yes, she is very troubled. Did you know that she saw an apparition?'

Simon shakes his head slowly.

'It was after the funeral. I wondered if Charles wasn't ready to leave; his death was very sudden.'

Simon creases his brow.

'She hasn't mentioned it since.'

The two men look at each other intently.

'I know she is distressed. Where did she see it?'

'She said there was one in the walled garden.' Dominic reaches out, puts his hand on his Bible on the desk, for comfort. His dear friend needs help.

Simon watches him, glad that they are sharing this burden.

'It certainly needs careful handling.' What is he going to tell Angus? 'You did the right thing. I'll make sure it gets into the right hands.'

Simon nods.

Dominic pushes the revolver to the back of a drawer and rings the bell for tea. Simon seems to relax as he drinks. It's obvious to Dominic that Simon, despite some of his apparent left-wing leanings, is anxious to help the Fairweathers as much as possible.

After Simon leaves, Dominic pours himself a stiff whisky. Practicality now. Speed and discretion are needed. The Diplomatic Service must handle this. He takes a sheet of notepaper and begins to write.

Leaving the palace, Simon's spirits are lifted by the sound of a Bach fugue coming from the cathedral, obviously the organ scholar practising. His stride lengthens as he makes his way towards the clear notes. Opening the heavy door, he stops to listen, breathing in the familiar smell of wax and incense. The air is cool. Candles are flickering, taking the prayers of his fellow men and women. He kneels in the nearest pew, his mind on Elspeth. May I find the right words for all people who come to me seeking Your comfort. His eyes stray up to the fan structures in the stone roof above. Men had constructed this amazing building, without modern tools, to honour God, to revel in His love.

Love, that is the word. He can feel it all around him, coming from the stone walls and ceiling and rising from the floor. Elspeth's reaction, staring at him intently, during the sermon when he quoted "thou shalt not kill" pops into his mind. Has she used the gun? He can't think that.

His thoughts turn to Auntie Vi; he can't really mention this to her. Not unless Elspeth wants him to, and he's reluctant to pry into her business. But all his flock need compassion.

45

Angus frowns. Who is that with Ma, talking so animatedly? He pulls Nancy to a halt and dismounts. Another Foreign Office official prying around? He walks the pony into the paddock. He'll rub him down soon. He needs to make sure Ma isn't being hassled again. Why don't they leave her alone? Another cleric? He looks a pleasant enough young chap, but he doesn't trust the Foreign Office. It would be another good cover, although why use clerics twice?

Are they looking for the statue that makes Mother anxious? He stiffens; he has always dreaded it might be connected with the horse that he bought and exported. What it is to have a complicated history. Not of his own making either. He was very surprised by the request, but he knows the Diplomatic Service has many hidden ways of influencing foreign policy.

Taking a deep breath, he strolls across to the terrace. If he needs to send the fellow on his way, he'll do it courteously but firmly.

'Hello, Ma. Is everything all right?'

She smiles at her son. 'Oh, Angus, meet Kris, the new curate.'

‘I’ve brought some books that I think will be useful.’ He passes them to Elspeth. ‘Hinduism, some early Buddhist discourses and the other one I mentioned.’

‘Oh, you must be a free thinker.’ Angus shakes his hand.

Kris grins.

46

Elspeth finishes her coffee, folds the Telegraph. It's no good, she can't concentrate. She walks across the room, looks out of the window, blankly. She knows Dominic wants to help her, but she has a feeling that she can't be helped. He wants her to be happy. He is always kind and gentle. She gives herself a little shake. This isn't the way. Get ready, be accepting of help.

Gertrude comes in to clear the breakfast table.

'It's a lovely day' she says, 'too nice to be inside.'

. 'Yes, it is. I'm going to walk down to the village to return a book.'

Kris is waiting on the doorstep ready to welcome her.

'Lady Fairweather, please come in'.

An incense stick is burning in the living room, there are books everywhere, a stack on the round table in the bay window, others in piles on the floor.

'Do sit down.' He gestures towards a blue velvet sofa across the room.

Still holding the book, she threads her way carefully through the clutter and sinks into the soft fabric, struggling to sit upright. 'Taking the marker out of the slim volume she points to the page. 'I found this fascinating.

He takes the book. 'Ah, exorcism. I've had training in that but have never had the opportunity to carry one out.' He lowers himself into an armchair opposite her. 'I would like to hear more about your experience.'

Elspeth closes her eyes; it will be a relief to tell someone about all the scenes which keep playing in her mind. The walled garden was where it started.

'It was in the evening, after Charles' funeral.'

Kris sits quietly. nodding occasionally as she recalls each incident. As she goes on, she begins to tense.

'Is the spirit listening now?'

'Possibly.'

'Are you able to help me?'

'He needs to go to the Light. I marvel at the way you have kept these visitations to yourself. 'I am very willing to do an exorcism if you would like me to.' He picks up another book. 'This gives a more detailed account of the process.'

Can she trust this young man? She can see the earnest look on his face. He seems sincere. 'Thank you. That will be helpful.'

Closing the gate of Primrose Villa behind her, Elspeth is pleased that she opted to walk. It will give her thinking time before being accosted by Gertrude's concern. She's looking forward to reading about the removal of apparitions, ghosts or whatever it is. She holds the book in front of her with both hands, to look at the cover.

Will the damned ghost really go? Is it possible? She turns to walk back up the road. Glancing across at Huw's cottage, she wonders if he has seen her. He is nowhere in sight.

As she reaches the point in the road where the houses give way to fields on one side and the church on the other, a car appears. It almost stops by the sign of Whistledon-on-Wye, then heads towards her, stopping and starting outside each cottage; she realises the driver is reading the names on the gates. The village postman doesn't need numbers, but it can be awkward for visitors.

As the car nears her, Elspeth sees it has a foreign number plate. She smiles at the driver, who draws alongside and, in a French accent, asks if she can tell her which is Willow Cottage. Surprised, Elspeth says,

'Oh, you must have come to see Huw Lloyd. It's the one with the thatched roof over there.' Elspeth is breathing heavily. A French woman going to Huw's, and he was away all that time in France, saying his visit was related to work. Maybe she's come to look at St Asaph's, to discuss the twinning, but why visit Willow Cottage? Elspeth watches the car turn into the drive. Who is she? Her legs turn to jelly; she forces them one in front of the other, until she reaches the Lodge. She's short of breath, stands for a moment, holding the fence, her mind whirling. She doesn't really know him. All this "get to know each other" has been very one-sided. She's having nothing more to do with the canon. Did the F.O. really send him, or is he simply a terrible man after what he can get? She takes a deep breath, anger rising, draws herself up, begins to walk quickly up the drive.

'Rat, rat, rat,' she says under her breath, keeping pace with her steps. That French woman looked very pleased with herself.

By the time she reaches the Hall, Elspeth is seething. She's been duped. She must forget him. Enough is enough. She goes quickly upstairs before anyone can see her tear-stained cheeks, throws herself on the bed and sobs.

47

Thoughts of Monique's compliant body against his are becoming increasingly frequent. Huw caresses himself gently. She has a very persuasive touch that can move him slowly to a wonderful intensity. He's pleased to have a rest from Elspeth. Her anxiety is a hindrance; he is not being satisfied, and neither is he making any progress in his enquiries.

Cathedral Close
St Asaph
Ma Cherie,

I wish that I could have been with you for your retirement celebration. It was certainly well-deserved after all your years of service. Life with you in St Amand cannot come soon enough. I have started the application for French citizenship. Of course, I will still have some duties at the Cathedral and may have to leave you occasionally for a week or two.

My current assignment is a delicate one, but I hope to be free to travel soon.

Je t'envoie tout mon amour,

Huw

He leans back, puts down his pen, then sits up again as a car draws into the driveway. He knows that blue Citroën. How did Monique find him here? He looks down at the letter on the table with St Asaph's as a heading. He takes a drink from the glass of beer next to it, then screws up the paper and throws it into the waste-paper basket. Whatever is she doing here? His mind scurries in all directions as he goes out to greet her.

He pauses in the doorway as she eases herself out of the car, giving him a tired smile.

'Ma Cherie, what a lovely surprise.' How has she found him? 'Let me get your bags.'

'Huw, I am exhausted. I've had to drive much further than I expected. Why didn't you tell me where you were?'

He carries her bags into the hallway, embracing her and stilling her questions with a kiss. 'Confidentiality, Cherie, I am working.'

48

Elspeth's eyes are drawn to the hawthorn tree, her marker for the hiding place. Is the rain beginning to ease? She can't go out in this pouring rain, risk drawing attention to herself. Her heart pounds in her ears, she needs to know that it is safe. She can't get away from the thought that the gun is a magnet, can draw any random walker. She imagines someone finding it, using it to shoot the horses, to threaten Gertrude or perhaps take it to the police. She cringes, can see herself on trial in Newport Crown Court. Is there a faint sun showing through the clouds, is it clearing?

Half-an-hour later she pulls on her coat and boots and sets off across the sodden grass. The river is high, the ground saturated, it has rained and rained all week. Nearing the tree, she picks her way through the mud. Slithering about, her boots become caked in the heavy earth. She steadies herself with the firm stones and soggy moss of the wall, dodges the thorny twigs of the tree, until she comes to the familiar triangular loose stone. Her heart races, it must be there. She wishes she had thrown it away immediately, but in her panic, she'd been unable to think of any way or anywhere to do it, without being seen. Now it is a liability. She can't leave it to lie there any longer.

Taking a deep breath, she carefully removes the stone, closes her eyes and plunges her hand into the cavity. Her wet fingers probing the space can feel nothing except rough, hard stone on all sides. The hole is empty. It has gone, disappeared, been taken. Her legs wobble beneath her. Huw has found it! He must have been watching her; but what if Huw hasn't taken it? Who has? Is someone still watching her? Elspeth staggers. Waves are crashing around in her head; rocks are being thrown at her. She feels the violence of a storm shaking her to the very core. She closes her eyes, hangs onto the wall, clutches at the thorny branches, grasps the rough trunk of the tree.

What can she do? Breathe. Breathe. Conscious breathing, mindfulness. She opens her eyes and looks up through the tree's branches. The sky is still full of dark grey clouds, but a pale sun has appeared. A blackbird flies into the tree above and begins to sing.

A rasping sound disturbs her. The hinges of the blue churchyard-door need oiling. She can hear the barking of dogs, the door opening and closing, then footsteps passing along the path towards the river. She keeps as still as she can. She will deny it. She must not be seen. She must brazen it out. She does not need to admit to anything.

Waiting until she is sure that the person is far enough away, she straightens herself, and with deliberate strides, makes her way back to the Hall.

Elspeth can hear Gertrude singing as she polishes the furniture in the dining room. It jars on her ears. Leaving her muddy boots by the front door, she quickly climbs the stairs to her room. She can't be seen to be agitated again. Oh, why has she been stupidly careless? She's been so anxious to check on the gun's presence, she hasn't bothered to wear gloves. The gun will have its own fingerprint too. Diplomatic immunity is all she can pray for. Charles. Charles. Why? Why aren't you here?

She sleeps fitfully that night. Short bouts of sleep with vivid dreams. Staircases to climb and descend. Roads which go nowhere but are familiar too. Hooded men in dark clothes hiding in doorways. In between the dreams, she walks to the window, the river is shining in the moonlight. With cold feet, she pads back to wrap herself tightly in the bedclothes.

Dawn comes and she drops into a deep sleep, only stirring when she hears Gertrude knocking on her door.

49

Angus looks around the bar for the new curate. Sees him, a pint in hand, talking with a group of teenagers. He's ordering his drink when Kris turns, grins at him, gives one of the group a friendly pat and comes hurrying across. 'Sorry about that.'

Angus leads him over to a table in the corner, sets his pint carefully onto a beer mat, rubs his chin.

'It's about Ma. I believe you're helping her.' He pauses, purses his lips, looking at Kris with a quizzical expression. 'I don't know what you've told her, but she's been in a very strange mood since she visited you.'

Kris sits up, raises his eyebrows then frowns. 'She seemed ok when she left.'

'Well, when she got back, she went straight to her room and was late coming to lunch. She looked as if she'd been crying.'

Kris looks at him intently. 'I don't think I said anything to trouble her.'

Angus looks at the young fellow. 'I'm not sure it's a good idea for her to visit you.'

He wipes his mouth on his sleeve. 'It was the rector's idea. She did say she's coming again next week.'

'I see. Well, any problems, just let me know.'

‘Of course.’

‘I guess we'll just see how it goes.’

50

The post has arrived. There is a letter with familiar writing on top of the pile. Huw's. She doesn't want to deal with it. But she must. Tentatively, she slits the envelope.

Willow Cottage

River Lane

My dearest Elspeth,

How I wish there were speedier ways to arrange our meetings. I am deeply sorry I couldn't see you before I left for France. When I returned and found your letter, I was greatly disturbed by the thought of you waiting pointlessly. Be assured I will be by the beech trees on Monday at 11a.m, eagerly waiting to hold you close.

I do hope you have been able to book the cottage in Rock as it looks as though my duties will require travel abroad for the remainder of the month. It is disappointing but unavoidable; I know you will understand.

I long to see you.

Yours,

Huw

Meet him by the beech trees? Not in a million years.

Huw frowns, why hasn't he heard from Elspeth? He should have pursued her more eagerly. He hasn't got the answers he needs. He'd felt he was about to get the information the F.O. wants. Has there been the suggested bribery? A racehorse is certainly possible. The Greek statue, he'd walked the gardens and park looking for that. Of course, it might not be on show. As to the gun. Is there one?

He must try again. Does he need to threaten her with disclosure of his task, say he knows she has a gun and that there will be someone coming to search for it? She might be frightened into sharing all that she knows. He pauses in his walk. He needs to act soon. He hastens back to Willow Cottage.

Heart thumping, Elspeth bristles as she picks up the letter. She can feel Gertrude's eyes boring through her back. What's this about? She doesn't want any contact with him.

Breathing deeply, she climbs the stairs as calmly and deliberately as she is able. In her bedroom, she leans against the closed door, the letter feeling alive in her taut hands.

Crossing to her desk, she grabs the paperknife and slits the envelope, recoiling as she reads.

My dear Elspeth,

As you know, I was sent to Istanbul to counsel you, which I believe I did successfully. I must confess that I may have strayed beyond my remit, but you are extremely alluring. I need to confess, as well, to having a professional interest in the shootings.

May I suggest that we meet in the little church at Nether Whistledon at 11 o'clock tomorrow. It's very small and only open for visitors to view the old wall paintings. It would be a perfect place to put an end to the terrible consequences of your time in Istanbul.

Yours as ever,

Huw

Huw wants to meet. She won't. But does she need to defend Charles' reputation? Her eyes fix on the neat handwriting. The tight script of a control freak. He's trapped her. Why did she trust him? What has she said? Her mind flicks back to one evening in the cottage. Did she hint that Charles had been negotiating privately with the consul?

Memories flood into her mind, the smiling face of his wife, the black hair, the white teeth, very attractive, enticing! Tears of anger trickle down her cheeks. It's a complete mess. Charles didn't tell her much. She couldn't have given Huw any details.

She must pull herself together. She hates herself for the jealous, 'poor me' thoughts that she'd indulged in.

Charles had been a good man and a good husband and father; she will meet Huw and convince him of Charles' innocence.

She looks at herself in the mirror. Determinedly smiling, she takes her powder puff. dusts her nose and cheeks. Gertrude will not see that she has been crying.

51

Elspeth realises she's being frosty with everyone. She was very short with Gertrude when she came to ask about lunch. Is she really so anxious about meeting Huw or is she just making sure that she doesn't give him the wrong signals?

She dresses as casually as she can and, with just a dash of lipstick for makeup, sets off towards the paddock. Ezra whinnies a welcome and nuzzles against her shoulder as she leads him towards the stables.

The road up from Nether Whistledon is steeper and more winding than Elspeth remembers. Ezra plods stoically up the deserted road. Listening to his hooves ringing out in the silence, she feels very alone. Is she riding into battle? She straightens her back, she can deal with this man, now that she sees him for what he is.

Huw has not slept well. His shaving mirror tells him he is not looking his best. His face is drawn and there are dark circles under his eyes. He will be pleased when this case is wrapped up. Life with Monique will be a blessed relief. There comes a time in most investigations when it's necessary to step back and make a final report. Elspeth hasn't been easy to fathom. She doesn't seem to know the difference between fiction and fact.

He pulls on his walking shirt and trousers, tucks his recording pen into the shirt pocket, then dons his cagoule.

The early morning mist is still lingering as he sets off up the hill. The little church is five miles away but will be perfect for his purpose. Very few people visit. They can sit in comfort and be warm and dry. The acoustics will help with the clarity of his recording.

The sun is beating down. Elspeth urges Ezra on. Looking over the dusty hedge to her left, she sees the little church with its squat tower. They continue up the road to a wooden gate.

Leading him through, she ties the reins to a young ash tree at the top of the sloping field; he begins nibbling the long grass. She walks down the mown path to the porch.

She has seen no-one for the last half hour. Has Huw arrived before her? She lifts the metal latch, the heavy door squeaks as she pushes it open; the cool damp air meets her as she steps inside.

The church is empty. She recoils at the sight of the rood screen. It is blood red. She drops onto a wooden pew, closes her eyes to shut it out. Memories tumble through her, weaken her. She opens and closes her fists, searching for the determination she had earlier.

A hand on her shoulder frightens her. She shrinks from the touch. Turns, unsmiling, meets Huw's gaze.

'What do you want?'

Huw's lips are pressed into a smile.

'I'm here to help you, Elspeth. We just need to clear a few things up.'

'Have you got it?'

He frowns. 'What do you mean? Have I got what?'

She looks at him through narrowed eyes. 'Then just leave me alone. I don't need your help anymore.'

He takes her hand; she doesn't resist or respond to his pressure.

'I suggested we meet here, in this ancient haven of prayer, so that you'll be able to give your problems to God and leave comforted.'

Her eyes lock on his. He really doesn't know her... but if it means he'll leave her alone... She bows her head.

Standing over her, he intones a prayer.

If only priests spoke normally, the words might feel more genuine. The ritual over, she thanks him and makes ready to leave.

'Perhaps we could run through a few things now...'

She needs air, gets up, pushes past him, reaches for the door handle, but his hand is there, keeping the door firmly closed. The missing gun is her only thought. Why didn't she get rid of it sooner? Who's taken it? She won't be blackmailed. She will deny all knowledge. If necessary, she'll take the consequences. Charles had always said, "give in to blackmail and you are never free."

'Huw, let me go please.'

'I need to talk to you about several things. Shall we sit down again?'

'Who sent you? I don't think you are who you said you are.'

'Elspeth, I was sent by the Foreign Office to investigate what happened; I confess that when I met you, it became different. You are very attractive, and I thought you had feelings for me too. Perhaps, if you are open with me about everything, we can start again.'

Elspeth laughs and looks away.

His hand rests on her shoulder; she allows it to stay.

'Think about it, my dear. I will be in contact with you, very soon. We can bring this to a close and be free to enjoy each other's company again.'

Elspeth hears his footsteps disappearing. The gun is lost. It can incriminate her. Charles had succumbed to personal bribery. The ghost is telling her that it's all going to end badly. Outside, in the churchyard, Ezra whinnies.

52

Elspeth can stand it no longer: the haunting memories of Istanbul, the apparition, that menace of a man. Is there no escape from this torment? She walks across the parkland; St Peters is visible through the trees. Can she find quiet in there? Can she find comfort anywhere?

She takes the path leading to the blue door and goes through into the churchyard. The yew trees are welcoming her, their branches heavy from the recent shower of rain; the gravestones, as always, remind her of the Fairweathers of long ago; some must have suffered too. She hovers, tentative. Then, in her flimsy shoes, makes her way across to Charles' grave. The newly erected marble headstone shining. She brushes against the leaves, raindrops soaking into her thin jacket, her feet wet from the sodden grass. She reads the inscription:

"Charles Fairweather, beloved husband of Elspeth". She feels bereft. He would have known what to do. She touches the stone, willing him to give her some guidance. Does he know that she'd used his gun? Does he know that she'd hidden it in the wall behind the hawthorn? Does he know it's disappeared? She waits for a sign of some sort, some guidance from Charles, she looks about, listens. She can hear footsteps coming towards her, crunching on the gravel path. She looks up. It's the rector, Simon, walking towards her, smiling, but it's not his usual smile. She finds the expression difficult to read.

'Lady Fairweather - Elspeth - I think I have found something of yours. It is now in a safe place.'

Elspeth clutches the top of the gravestone, swaying as she realises what he's saying, she can barely breathe.

He takes her hand, leads her to the church.

As he opens the door, the pungent perfume of lilies assails her; suddenly blinded by tears, she moves towards the altar. The cross is gleaming. Simon kneels beside her. His quietly spoken prayer is comforting; gradually, her despair ebbs as a feeling of calm sweeps through her.

The walk back to the Hall seems long. Passing the paddock, Elspeth rests, looking over the gate. Ezra comes towards her, nuzzles her hand. She strokes him, tears flowing down her cheeks. He loves her although she has done terrible things. She is safe with him, safe from everything. The gun is in a safe place. What did Simon mean when he said that? It didn't sound as if he had reported it to the authorities. She didn't care what they thought, they hadn't been in her position. Who knew what they would have done? Had he told Dominic? Would they tell Kris? She needs his friendship. She must make sure Angus doesn't find out; he won't handle it well. He'd coped with his father's bribery but there was no need for him to know about her role in the events. Where was the apparition now? Had he gone with the gun? This was another reason she had hidden it outside; so that the spectre would not come into the Hall. She must compose herself before going back inside. She dries her eyes, feeling the comfort of her horse.

53

Elspeth stands on the terrace, relishing the balmy air as she waits for Kris. It's a perfect evening for their meditation. Will he be able to lead her into finding the spark in her that feels eternal? Or is she beyond help?

She sees him, walking towards her, smiling calmly.

He looks directly into her eyes, briefly puts his hand on her arm. 'Would you like to lead the way?'

She nods. 'I'm so looking forward to it.' She takes him through the grounds, towards the rose garden, breathing in the sweet fragrance of night scented stock.

He's beside her, apparently enjoying the tranquillity.

They reach the trellising where roses tumble and trail, then continue into the garden with its blooms of beautiful red, pink, yellow and white roses. They pause, inhaling the perfect perfume from each variety.

As they near their intended seat, Elspeth gasps, stops. In the middle of the dried-up lily pool is the statue.

Kris jogs ahead, rubs his hand over the marble. 'What a marvellous statue. How lucky you are to have it.'

Ashen faced, she shakes her head, sinks down onto the stone bench.

54

Huw is enjoying Monique's company. Reluctantly, he makes an appointment to see Elspeth. He really doesn't want the hassle of Elspeth and her troubled mind. But he does want his pension. The F.O. will be awkward if he doesn't produce results. If it wasn't for that, he would have left this village by now. Everyone seems to know each other. How is he supposed to keep matters confidential?

Elspeth hears the doorbell. She is aware that she is straightening to her full height. That will be Huw, exactly on time. She stands waiting for Gertrude to show him into the room, a formal smile on her lips. She will make sure this is a short meeting and to the point. Whatever his point is. Does he know that she saw his French visitor arrive? She should never have fallen for his charming persuasion. She cannot see how she has allowed herself to do so. He was a clergyman and should have been counselling forgiveness. She was in shock of course, didn't think straight.

None of this would have happened if Charles hadn't been stupidly attracted to that woman. Then she'd been stupidly attracted to this man.

It is taking Gertrude a long time to answer the door. That is good, keep the man waiting. He was most unpleasant when they were in the little church, almost threatening. She is not going to tell him anything. Today, she will feign ignorance.

She takes a deep breath as Gertrude ushers Huw into the room.

'Good morning, Huw. How can I help you?'

'Good morning, Elspeth. As much as I regret having to raise the subject again, I'm afraid there are still questions to be answered. The Foreign Office is concerned for the lives of the team in Istanbul. The main problem is that there has been a lot of talk about the shootings; this doesn't make for good diplomatic relations. The F.O. feel that if they can give reassurance that the culprit has been punished, it will restore the relationship.'

'But I am unable to help you.'

'Do you have Charles' gun?'

'No, Huw, I don't.'

'There was talk of bribery.'

'What are you saying, Huw? That my husband was less than an honourable man?'

'If I don't give them the answers they need, they may want to question you in person.'

Is he threatening her again? Who does he think he is?

'Huw, there is nothing more I can add to what I've told you. If that is all you have come for, I'll bid you goodbye.'

Huw stood his ground. 'I don't think that we can leave it just like that, Elspeth. I thought that we had a better relationship than this. I was sent to help you, and I still want to do so. Can we sit down and talk properly?'

'I might have been able to if I hadn't felt threatened by you when we were in the little church and if I hadn't met that very attractive French blonde, who I'm told is staying at your cottage.'

Huw took a step back. 'I don't think you understand everything. But as you feel like that, I must just pass my unverified findings to the F.O. You will see what they think. It is out of my hands now and into theirs. I will go. I am sorry that our relationship has ended like this.'

She glares at him as she rings the bell. The housekeeper is soon there. 'Gertrude, please will you show Canon Lloyd out.'

Huw, a smile fixed on his face, follows the housekeeper.

55

Kris, standing waiting for Elspeth to arrive, sees the man across the road emerge wearing a casual shirt, carry two large suitcases to the car. He puts them down, opens the boot and hoists them in. Smiling, he slams the lid. Taking some keys out of his trouser pocket, he locks the cottage door and pushes them through the letterbox. Getting in the car, he drives away, following the Citroen.

Elspeth, every cell in her body tingling after her brisk walk, focuses her attention on the garden of Primrose Villa, avoiding looking towards Willow Cottage. Is Huw watching her?

Meeting her at the door, Kris leads her into the room and gestures. 'Do sit down, Elspeth.'

He has rearranged the room. The furniture is pushed back; the floor is clear. Two upright chairs are in the centre of a large round rug. She takes one, sits fondling her pearl necklace, feeling the smooth round beads one by one.

'Remember, Elspeth. You are safe. I want you to invite the apparition to sit on the other chair opposite you. We can help his trapped soul to transition to the light. Be calm, send him love.'

She closes her eyes, puts her hands in her lap, tilts her head forward, waiting.

He speaks quietly. 'Think of the man. Remember all the times you saw him, how he kept his distance, never intruded, never tried to harm you. Imagine him sitting there opposite you.'

She concentrates. Deep brown eyes are gazing at her, a face, then a hazy figure appears.

Kris' voice breaks in. 'He is asking for forgiveness.'

She opens her eyes.

'Keep your concentration. He wants you to know he will have to stay in the Earth realm until you forgive him. He says Charles has forgiven him already.' Kris holds her gaze, inclines his head.

'It's no good, I can't do it.'

'Elspeth, remember that you are here to help him. He's trapped. He has been asking you for two years.'

'He's been following me, traumatising me. As if it were not enough for him to kill Charles.' She sighs heavily.

'If you want him to leave you alone, forgiveness is the only way.' He spreads his arms wide, sending energy towards her.

Elspeth can hear the kindness and patience in Kris's voice. He's right, she feels her resistance draining away. Please forgive me, too. Then, in a strong, clear voice, says, 'I forgive you.'

Kris is quiet for a few moments then says, 'Spirit, you are now free to go to the light.'

Elspeth senses an unseen hand touching her hair, as the scent of jasmine permeates the air. Opening her eyes, she smiles at Kris, blinking back tears.

Kris clasps his hands together, bows his head. 'Namaste.'

Elspeth responds, 'Namaste. I can't thank you enough.'

He remains still. 'Life is a marvellous experience.' He passes her a glass of water 'Take your time. I'll be back.'

She sips, welcomes the cool refreshing liquid, grounding her. She looks at the rug beneath her feet, a traditional Indian pattern, its swirls imprint in her mind, feels the upright wooden chair supporting her. Hearing Kris softly padding into the room, she swivels. He comes to stand beside her.

'You've really helped me.'

He puts his hand on her shoulder. 'I found it very moving, a privilege.'

Does he know? Her heart beats faster. 'I'm not ready to go home yet. I think I'll call into the church.'

'I'm going to see Simon. Shall we walk together?'

Elspeth nods, although she would rather be on her own; he's a good fellow and she doesn't want to seem rude.

They tread carefully; the pavement is uneven, tree roots have caused the tarmac to rise, the air is still. Is her life becoming better? If so, it's thanks to this young man. Dominic sent him. She looks at Kris walking beside her. He did well, it must have been difficult for him, he'd never done an exorcism before.

She smiles reassuringly. 'I do think he's gone. I feel different. You say that he's gone to the light. What does that mean?'

Kris glances at her sideways. 'Nobody really knows. Different religions have different ideas. It's a minefield. You will let me know if you need to talk any further about today's experience.'

Please, God, no. 'Thank you. That's most kind.'

56

As Simon sees Kris' smiling face, he beams.

'I gather the process was successful?'

'It seemed to go well. Elspeth forgave him and he disappeared. She didn't find it easy. She's gone into the church now to pray. She's calm but questioning where he went to. I find it difficult to explain. I don't know what you think.'

Simon scratches his head as he beckons Kris in.

'My Aunt Violet has been in touch with spirits for years, but it's never been for me. I think there's more turmoil than ever amongst the clergy. We are presented with all these scientific facts about light years and black holes. Life is very simple for those who have God sitting on a cloud but once we go to Darwin's theories...' He shrugs his shoulders.

Kris raises his eyebrows.

'I find it best to focus on the life of Jesus, how we need to follow his example.'

'I agree. The world would be a less troubled place if we all did that.'

'Tea?' He pauses. 'No, let's celebrate. Come on.' Heading to the living room, with Kris in tow, he delves in a cupboard, producing two glasses and two bottles of beer, quickly removing the tops with an opener, and pouring one carefully. 'Well done, you deserve this. Make yourself comfortable.'

'I hope you're right. Cheers.' He sits back onto the sofa, noticing through the window, that Claire is sitting on the patio.

'Only time will tell.' Simon sipping his beer, follows Kris' gaze.

'My wife enjoys the tranquillity of the garden, a restorative change from Church duties. I'm very lucky to have her help. As a young man I was full of enthusiasm for the job, but as time has gone by, I've come to find the Church to be divisive.'

Kris shifts. 'I am wondering if I've made the right choice. Recently I came across some information that claimed Jesus was a Buddhist monk.'

'I'm thinking about my Aunt Violet, she would have relished the opportunity to help but I didn't have the confidence to ask her. There's a lot for me to explore, so much that I don't understand. Can I do it from my position here?'

57

As Elspeth enters the church, the white altar cloth is suddenly tinted red and orange as the emerging sun shines through the old stained glass. Is this a sign? A strange feeling passes through her body; slowly her legs take her towards the family pew. She sinks to her knees onto the embroidered hassock, bows her head, waits until the tremor passes; sits back in the pew, spine straight, eyes fixed on a candlestick. Her mind is calming, gradually.

What does she believe? Was it really a trapped soul? Life and death are a mystery. The energy that was Charles, still is, so is that of the consul. They have both gone to the light. She feels spaced-out, needs to ground herself. She will walk into the woodland.

Amongst the trees, she breathes in the clean air, stands under an oak tree, hears the chatter of a jay. Flying away, its bright feathers cross her line of vision. She leans against the sturdy trunk feeling its stability and strength. She pats the rough bark. She is of this Earth, grounded; she is here for a purpose, whatever that might be.

Gertrude will be waiting to serve lunch.; she must hurry.

Gratitude floods through her body as she thinks of Angus and his venture. Charles would be proud of him, and she must be too. She can help him with the expense. She will buy a horse. She needs to look forward.

The sound of a bicycle bell brings her back to the present moment.

'Lady Fairweather, I've only one letter for the Hall today and it's for you. Can I give it to you now?' The postman reaches into his sack and pulls it out. 'It looks important. I wouldn't have given it to anyone else.'

Elspeth puts out her hand for the crisp, cream envelope, smiles her thanks.

Touching his cap, he gets back on his bike and disappears down the drive. She watches him go, looks at the envelope. It's from the F O. What now? What has Huw told them? She pushes it into her pocket; she will read it in her room. She walks slowly up the drive, not aware of anything but the letter in her pocket.

Opening it, she finds an invitation to a meeting in Whitehall. Her heart sinks 'Bloody Hell!' What can this mean, have they proved the bribery, or has the discovery of the gun prompted it? It is not just an invitation. It is a summons!

58

Hearing the bell, Gertrude opens the back door, amazed to see Bill, hands full of gladioli, delphiniums, lavender, and roses.

'For the mistress.'

'How beautiful; they aren't the same here now you've left.'

He nods knowingly. 'Got to give them love, you have.'

'Come in. 'I'll see if she's free.'

Bill looks around the kitchen. It hasn't changed in all the years he's known it.

Gertrude finds Elspeth in the conservatory, reading the Racing News.

'It's Bill. With flowers.'

Elspeth's eyes light up as he enters with the bouquet. He's combed his wiry hair, put on a tie, slightly askew.

'I heard you're in a spot of bother. Wanted to cheer you up and say... well, good luck.'

Elspeth drops the paper onto her lap, and takes the flowers, burying her nose in the roses, before breathing in the calming scent of lavender. 'Bill, thank you. I'm not sure what you've been told.'

‘Only that you’ve got to go to London.’ He looks down at his shoes, and then up at her. ‘If it's about that foreign crate…’

‘No, no. You weren’t to know what it was.’

He nods. ‘Well, whatever it is, I hope it turns out ok.’

59

Grey pigeons merge with the overcast sky. Simon lifts his collar up against the damp morning air. His mind is on Elspeth being driven to the Foreign Office by Dominic. She had seemed a little anxious yesterday; understandable, as the visit will be rekindling the trauma of Charles' assassination. It is good that Dominic is with her, he will be a comforting companion.

The dogs, eager to start the day, pull on their leads.

Elspeth gazes at the high ornate ceiling, the chandelier sparkling, each drop reflecting the golden light. Her gaze moves back to the smiling face of the man sitting opposite her. It shifts again to the flat worn brogues on her feet. She has let herself go. She realises now. How has it happened?

His voice goes on. 'Our man discovered... consul... to a faction...planning a coup. No intention... Oil Agreement.'

She is finding it difficult to concentrate, to follow his words. 'Gratitude, service to the country, a posthumous recognition of one of the unsung heroes of the Diplomatic Service.'

Charles would be pleased.

He continues, 'As his devoted wife, you have our gratitude for all that you have done.'

Epilogue

It is the first time that she has attended an auction, never mind joining in the bidding. Elspeth feels Dominic's firm hand under her arm, easing their way through the throng. He has the same confident ability to make his way to the front, that she found useful in Charles. Standing by the rail, she scrutinises the stallion being displayed. He nickers, shakes his head showing his teeth, swishing his tail as he paws the ground. Strong muscles in his haunches ripple under the shining dappled coat. She breathes in the mixed aroma of horses and men, as a flat-capped fellow next to her pulls on his pipe. She's not looking for a stud horse. If she were this would be a candidate. She smiles at Dominic. 'He looks the part.'

'Not what we need yet. The day will come, I'm sure. Wait!'

The young ones are due soon. She shifts her weight from foot to foot as a duel between bidders goes on, the price goes up and up.

Dominic seems to know what she's thinking.

'Don't worry,' he says 'We're in the market for untested animals. We may lose if they don't perform, but not as much. One day we might have a proven stallion to sell.'

Elspeth looks up at Dominic, his usual calm, affable face is filled with purpose and excitement.

'You are amazing. I had no idea you were so keen on the venture.'

'If I'm doing something, I need to do it well. Besides, I've always felt an affinity with horses.'

The people in the crowd around seem to have no idea this man is a bishop. He certainly knows his horses and which ones are worth bidding for. She is much less sure but is happy to trust in his judgment.

The auctioneer, a stout fellow with a pleasant round red face, is introducing a young chestnut foal; he certainly looks promising. He has good proportions and, thinks Elspeth, extremely elegant legs. She likes Dominic's idea of buying two horses between them, instead of one each. It will be twice the excitement when they are racing, and both will benefit from hedging their bets.

He is going to do the bidding for the first one and then, if she wishes, she can bid for the next. It's another challenge she needs to overcome. She decides to buy a foal with the prospects of breeding.

Dominic is astute. He comes in quite late with his offer and almost immediately the deal is done. 'Now it's your turn' he says.

A small black filly with a star on her forehead comes prancing into the ring. Elspeth nods her approval. She can help Angus instead of feeling that she is a nuisance on his periphery. The sale goes well; she is surprised how confident she feels and sounds.

'Sold to Lady Fairweather' the words echo in her ears.

It is such a restful scene, looking over the paddock towards the river, sheep nibbling the grass, the church tower in the distance, peeking out over the yew trees. Thank you, Charles, thank you for everything you have been to me and for giving me this beautiful place to live. The familiar dull ache lands near her heart. How long is it going to take? Perhaps now that she is becoming involved in Angus' project, the pain might diminish. Today was stimulating and she is delighted with her purchase. The next thing to do is to name the filly. She is beautiful, Belle.

Elspeth lies on her bed reliving the day. Dominic was such a surprise; she thought he'd even surprised himself. He seems more than willing to visit their horses every month, and she has the idea that he'd be here more often, if his ecclesiastical duties permitted. Has he decided on the name yet? What did he say? Zadok, she really likes that. Perhaps Domino would be a good name. What's in a name anyway? She must just find a name that is easy to call, or to shout at the races. It would be good if the filly's name and the foal's name are similar and connected with the stables. Whistledon something.

About Bryn Berry

Bryn Berry is the pseudonym of sisters Margaret Tasker and Sonia Ingamells, nee Booth born in Doncaster, Yorkshire.

Margaret lives in Nottinghamshire and Sonia in Wales, 200 miles apart, but Covid lockdown brought them closer together by Email and WhatsApp.

The story began with an online creative writing course in which the task was to write a letter to an anonymous someone.

Margaret wrote from Upper Whistledon Hall, as Sir Angus Fairweather, the response by Sonia, was from Simon Shorthouse, the rector of the village church.

Solitary walks in the woods or by the beach gave space for problems to be created and countering solutions to arise.

With freedom, came the idea that they might have the makings of a book in their hands. Jessica kindly read the first draft and said she thought they had the bare bones of a novel. It has taken many happy hours to build the skeleton and flesh it out.

Twists and turns, aided by Jackie and Heather, have included changes of tense and points of view. It has been a fascinating process which has enriched the lives of both sisters.

We hope you enjoyed this book and if you have a moment to spare, we would very much appreciate a review on / at the store where you bought the book.

Thank you.

Email:
brynberry@brynberry.com

Printed in Dunstable, United Kingdom

75433815R00159